Mike & Roxie's
Vegetable Paradise

TIPS, TALES & OTHER BRAVE STORIES
ABOUT GROWING FOOD IN KANSAS CITY

BY MIKE HENDRICKS
& ROXIE HAMMILL

Good luck with! the rabbits

Roxie & Mike

KANSAS CITY STAR
BOOKS

Mike & Roxie's Vegetable Paradise
Tips, Tales & Other Brave Stories About Growing Food in Kansas City
By Mike Hendricks & Roxie Hammill

Editor: Gail Borelli
Designer: Amy Robertson
Photographer: Aaron Leimkuehler
Illustrator: Lon Eric Craven
Copy editor: Les Weatherford

Published by
Kansas City Star Books
1729 Grand Boulevard
Kansas City, Mo. 64108
Kansascity.com

First edition

ISBN 978-1-933466-93-4

Library of Congress Control Number: 2009935614

Printed in the United States of America by Walsworth Publishing Inc., Marceline, Mo.

 **KANSAS CITY STAR BOOKS**

Contents

How To...

Acknowledgments

We are grateful to the many people who helped in the making of this book: Gail Borelli, for her careful and astute editing; Amy Robertson, for her wonderful design work; Les Weatherford, for his conscientious copy-editing; and photographer Aaron Leimkuehler, for making it all look great. We also owe our thanks to Doug Weaver of Star Books for his support of the project from the outset.

Thanks also to the people who kindly took time out from their normal schedules to be interviewed for this book: Chris Conatser, who showed us edible weeds; Lew Edmister; Brooke Salvaggio; Steve Mann; Powell Gardens horticulturists Alan Branhagen, Matt Bunch and Barbara Fetchenhier; and Dan Leap for letting us take a look at his rooftop container garden.

We've had a lot of help from gardeners over the years who have commiserated with us, shared their secrets and gently guided us away from disaster. Among them are horticulturists Dennis Patton and Chelsey Wasem at Johnson County K-State Research and Extension, the crew at the Johnson County Master Gardeners and all of our gardening neighbors over the years — Dorothy Christoph and her late husband, Leo; Genevieve Reeves and her late husband, Ken; Greg Ring; and Merle and Elaine Sparlin. A big thanks to Larry Verhaeghe and his grandmother, Eugenia Werbrouck, for letting us garden on their land all those years.

And, finally, thanks to Roxie's grandmother, Mildred Mears, who sowed the gardening seeds in her unwilling and ungrateful granddaughter so long ago.

Preface
The secret to gardening in Kansas City? Just relax.

Maybe by now you've salivated over a few gardening books, seen a few television shows. The garden rows are clean, perfectly straight, painstakingly mulched. The greenery shows nary a spot of leaf fungus or bite of a caterpillar larva. Smiling children wander in and pluck uniformly red tomatoes. The television host gently loosens the soil and up pops a nest of darling Easter egg-shaped new potatoes. You feel yourself tearing up.

Or maybe you've seen a commercial showing the dark side of seedsmanship. The man grimacing with lower back pain. The woman whose hands, useless as flippers, cannot seem to grasp the bedding plant and trowel. They throw down their tools in disgust and buy whatever labor-saving product is being advertised.

The truth is somewhere in the middle.

Yes, you can have a good garden. Maybe even a great one. But chances are it will never be as uniformly perfect as the ones on TV.

And, yes, it will be hard work. Sometimes you'll get sore. But unless you give up immediately and plow under the garden at the first sign of adversity, you will get something good out of it.

Following are some of the "dirty little secrets" of gardening in Kansas City that we've learned through the years. It may help to remember them as you toil:

• It might be a great year for some things some of the time, it might be an OK year for most things most of the time, but it will almost never be a great year for all things all of the time. We can think of only one year in our 25 years of gardening when everything was great. It was back in the late 1980s or early '90s.

• A lot of gardening has to do with luck. We know it's the American Way to give credit for hard work and determination, and they have their places in gardening. But that freak April hard freeze that lasted a week and killed all the tender pea and onion shoots? The bone-crushing drought lasting all spring and into July? Those were bad luck. Not your fault. Roll the dice again next year and things might be different.

• There are no garden police. If you have a few weeds, no lady in white gloves is going to shake her finger at you. To be sure, the weeds will impose their own discipline by not allowing you to have a good crop. But peer pressure should not enter into the mix.

• Gardening isn't as hard as TV commercials and the "Anal Retentive Gardening Show" make it sound. That's not to say there aren't frustrating moments. But don't be intimidated. You can put in a lot less work and still get a good garden. It won't be maximum yield. That's for later, when you become obsessive.

• The most important secret: You can mess up. Maybe you won't get the harvest of your dreams, but chances are you'll end up with something. Your plants want to survive. It's nature's way. Help them out even a little, and they'll do their best to thrive.

Hope that helps.

About us

ROXIE

When I was little, my grandmother had a garden in Jefferson, Iowa. It was a big plot with every vegetable you could think of, plus strawberries and black raspberries. She was always trying to get me to help her plant and pick, and once in a while I did.

Later, we'd sit at the table and my grandparents would exclaim over the garden produce. How it was much better than anything you could get at the grocery store. How the potatoes were "like butter" and the carrots "like candy." How you'd never go hungry if you could grow a garden.

Mostly, I ignored this. I was too young and inexperienced to appreciate the difference between a store tomato and garden-grown. And, after a few summers walking beans and detasseling corn, I sure wasn't going to spend my free time slaving away in the dirt. I figured a few dollars would buy me anything I wanted without the suffering, thank you very much. That darned Great Depression wasn't going to happen again, so why would I ever worry about going hungry?

How things can change.

My name is Roxie Hammill. I'm a writer and a piano teacher, and I've been gardening 25 years. I live in Lenexa, Kan., with my husband, Mike Hendricks, a longtime metro columnist for *The Kansas City Star*. We have three kids, Sam, Pete and Irene, who

have gardened with us — with differing levels of enthusiasm — from time to time.

I do all the garden chores that start with "p": planning, planting, picking, processing. In other words, all the important stuff. Mike does all the rest. I read the garden books, take notes on the shows and come up with the (sometimes) brilliant plans. He does the hard work. I am the evil Dr. Frankenstein. He is my beloved Igor.

It's been an arduous journey, but our brave little garden has stood us well. We started out small and suffered through droughts, floods, varmints and miserable failures. But we always ended up with something. And, yes, today we often talk about potatoes "like butter" and carrots "like candy."

So, ha, ha, Gram. The joke's on me.

MIKE

Yes, Roxie does all the "important stuff" — the stuff that wouldn't be possible if not for the efforts of her hard-working and devilishly handsome husband.

Before she can plant, someone has to roto-till. And then there's the composting, the manure spreading, the weeding, the harvesting of the root vegetables (involves digging), the setting up of the tomato cages, the making of the tomato cages — and on and on.

In other words, we have a nearly equal partnership going in our backyard garden paradise. She supplies the brains, and I supply the brawn — and sometimes the firepower.

Of course, it is against the law to fire a weapon — even one that shoots BBs — inside the city limits. But passersby have probably wondered about the man who sometimes appears on our back porch in his bathrobe and seems to take aim at the squirrels in the garden. I have no idea who that person might be, but I entirely understand his frustration.

As for my gardening credentials, I had none before marrying my co-author. Growing up in Omaha, Neb., the vegetables I ate came from the supermarket, and then only out of a can or a frozen box or bag. Maybe that's why I wasn't all that fond of them.

Now, however, I enjoy the fruits of our garden and take pride in the fact that, just maybe, I had a little something to do with filling our freezer and pantry with good things to eat.

Chapter 1:
It all started in 1985...

Not everyone can pinpoint the exact moment they grew up.

I can. It was a spring day in 1985. We had just moved to the Kansas City area and, in the process, gone from two incomes to one. I would stay home for a few years and take care of our 1-year-old.

It was a Saturday morning, and we had decided to go out and do something — maybe have breakfast and walk through a museum. As a double-earner family, we'd always been pretty free with our spending. So we didn't have a clue what our checking account balance was as we pulled up to the ATM.

The machine knew, though. Balance: $35. To last the next week.

I say this not to bring you down, but to point out that life can change randomly and without notice. One day we were a happy-go-lucky couple who thought nothing of dropping $60 on music. The next day we were packing lunches and washing out plastic bags. We had become Frugal.

Our first garden — a tiny plot at the back of our rented house in Roeland Park, Kan. — followed soon after.

There wasn't much room. We turned over some dirt along the chain-link fence, put in a couple of railroad ties and a little topsoil and *voila*! There was enough space for two or three tomato plants, a zucchini and a few green beans.

But we were hooked. The sight of our own food — that chemical-free food that cost us next to nothing — was powerful. When you've looked into the ATM and seen the abyss, there's nothing so soothing as food in the freezer.

When the season was over, we searched for a community garden space so we could have more room. We found a spot in Shawnee, Kan., and reserved two adjacent plots for a big garden. We planted everything: Garlic. Potatoes. Beans. Tomatoes, of course. Despite our many mistakes, that garden yielded enough that we had to buy a chest freezer.

Things changed again the next year. Shawnee decided to put a swimming pool and library where the community garden was. In the meantime, we bought a house with a yard so small there was no sunny space at all for a garden.

Never mind. After settling in, we noticed a large patch of unkempt ground across the street and down a couple of houses. This was the site of a formerly huge garden. The gentleman had passed away, but his elderly wife still lived in the house.

So we knocked on the door and did a deal. We'd mow the yard, which was sizable even without the garden, and in return get full use of the land in question.

5 good reasons to garden other than food BY ROXIE

There are plenty of practical reasons to garden: Low-cost groceries, a cleaner environment, untainted and fresh food. If you're considering your own garden, you probably already have your own list.

But let's forget "practical" for a moment and concentrate on "fun." A garden can be fun in all kinds of surprising ways:

1 **Your kids will have a lifetime supply of great stuff for Show and Tell.** Examples from our past include an animal molar (probably from a cow) and an old-time blue glass medicine bottle found in the soil.

2 **There's something so satisfying** about putting seeds in the ground and marveling at them as they grow and produce food. It sounds corny, but turning up that first big potato is like digging buried treasure. It never gets old.

3 **You will make friends.** I can't count the number of times someone has pulled up and shouted a question, or knocked on our back door. Many are curious or want to share a gardening tip or memory. You'll need those friends if you have excess produce you want to get rid of.

4 **You will marvel** at freaky, oddly shaped vegetables, such as a pair of carrots intertwined in a very Kama Sutra sort of way.

5 **You will learn to predict the weather.** You'll find yourself listening closely to all the explanations of cold fronts and isobars, maybe even arguing and talking back to the weather anchor. In the end, you, too, can look up at the fringe of a cloudy "anvil top" in the western sky and say with conviction, "Storm's a-comin'."

Roxie's Gram inspects the garden.

We now had a plot so big you could put a house on it. It was so big we didn't buy garlic, tomatoes or green beans for years. So big we had to call in someone with a tractor to plow it because our roto-tiller couldn't handle it all. We sowed and reaped happily for 12 years, filling the freezer, until times got good enough to move to a bigger house with a bigger yard, also in Lenexa, Kan.

That brings us to the present. We had to cut down a huge evergreen tree to get space and sun for our garden, but we kept on gardening through good times and bad. We have a room in the basement filled with jars of tomato puree, pickles and salsa, as well as a chest freezer packed with vegetables. Because when the hard times come, there's nothing so soothing as a larder fully stocked.

Comfort food, indeed.

Left: Roxie hauls
in some garden booty.
Opposite: Two brassicas
and two cute kids.

14

Chapter 2:
Finding your garden style

There are a lot of ways to garden if you are determined. It's possible to get a surprising amount of food from even a small bit of dirt, water and sun.

Following are some types of gardens, their pros and cons:

THE TRADITIONAL PLOWED-UNDER PLOT

This is the garden plan for you if you have a section of yard that gets a lot of sun and not much traffic. Ask yourself, "Would this be in the beeline my dog and/or kids make from the back door to the gate? Or the pool? Or the swing set?" If the answer is "yes," you might want to think again.

Pros: Since the garden is at ground level, you save on the expense of landscaping ties and other equipment needed for raised beds. The ground stays moist longer than with a container or raised bed, a big consideration in Kansas City where the hot summer winds blow.

You also can walk straight into a ground-level garden. There's no lifting of tillers or lawnmowers onto the dirt. (Lawnmowers, you ask? Well, yes. Occasionally we've been known to let things go, and, well, weeds happen.)

Cons: A big garden requires a big commitment. If you go out and do a little every day, it's manageable. Fun, even. But if a wet week is followed by a busy workweek and

Opposite: Size your garden to your needs and abilities. This size suits us best.

then a trip, you'll need to invest in gloves and bandages for the blisters. Also, you'll have to spend time processing all that food you'll be pulling in.

Some gardeners prefer raised beds; others like containers. Dan Leap's kiddie pool in Merriam, Kan., is a blend of both.

RAISED BEDS

This has become an increasingly popular way to garden. Typically, small plots are surrounded with landscaping ties or other building material and filled with topsoil.

Pros: The smaller beds are more manageable and easier to walk around than the large plot. And there's no denying they are prettier. The landscaping ties also give you something to sit on when weeding. (Warning: Pay attention to what type of construction material you use. Railroad ties, because of the chemicals used to treat them, are not recommended. Of course, we found this out after we'd already lined our first garden with railroad ties.)

Cons: All those ties and topsoil can get expensive. You can scour the area for construction trash and other free building stuff, but there's no guarantee you are going to get what you want when you want it. There's also the issue of finding a vehicle to haul everything.

18

Any time you put dirt in a raised container, be it a raised bed or a clay pot, the dirt tends to dry out and heat up faster. So raised beds, as a rule, need good mulching and more water. Also, it's easy to stub a toe and bark a shin as you chase squirrels through the raised-bed maze you've created.

CONTAINERS

Container gardening has gotten a lot of attention lately because it's city-friendly. Theoretically, you can have fresh tomatoes all summer, even if all the space you have is an apartment balcony.

Pros: Just about anything can be a container, from the traditional clay pot to the "topsy-turvy" upside-down tomato container—a recent innovation that has the plant growing from a hole in the bottom of a suspended bag. Some people have even been known to grow plants in a big bag of potting soil with holes punched here and there. K-State Research and Extension recommends 16-to-24-inch pots because they hold moisture longer and won't tip as easily in the wind.

Cons: In urban areas, too much sun reflecting off concrete and asphalt can damage plants (think scalded tomatoes). Plants also may refuse to set fruit as the highs go past about 90 degrees. Balconies and patios should offer some protection from overheating and wind damage.

Also, plants can drown without proper drainage. If you buy a pot from the garden store, be sure to pop out the drainage plugs on the bottom so water has somewhere to go. Not many plants like their roots to sit for days in soupy mud.

Lettuce for salads can be grown in a pot.

Homemade sugar tastes better in theory BY ROXIE

Ever had the urge to grow your own sugar?

Here is some advice: First buy a commercial-grade food processor. Then cover every kitchen surface with tarp. When you're all set up, go out for a drink and STAY THERE UNTIL THE URGE PASSES.

It started with a picture of a mangel in R.H. Shumway's seed catalog.

A mangel. Hmmm. That's interesting. What can you do with a mangel?

Well, according to the notes under the lumpy-looking root vegetable, a mangel is a type of beet with high sugar content. Must be another name for sugar beet, I assumed. Ergo, if I grew some, I could make my own sugar.

And it was on. My middle child was in grade school and needed a Learning Fair project. We had a 50-by-125-foot plot and plenty of room. So why not grow a few mangels?

It turned out to be one of our best garden years ever. Wheelbarrows full of tomatoes. Cauliflower as big as your head. And big, earthy, beautiful mangels the size of your forearm, if you are a muscular guy who's been working out.

Break out the corn flakes, kids! Mama's gonna put some homemade sugar on the table!

I hosed off the beets, got out my instructions and got busy.

The hides seemed fairly thick and bumpy, but, undaunted, I set to work with my little hand-held vegetable peeler. I got a surprise when I peeled away the first strip. The sugar beet was not red but a beautiful, dazzling white—the color of fresh snow.

"Look, Pete. Isn't this amazing? What a cool project this will be!"

As I peeled, the skins fell on a newspaper spread below. I peeled and peeled. Pete got bored and went to watch TV. When my hand began to get tired, I looked up and noticed: The peeled beets had started to turn an ugly, unappetizing gray.

This can't be right. Sugar is white.

To mitigate the color, I jumped into the next task: Chopping the beets and grinding them in a blender.

They turned an even more horrifying color as I chopped. By the time they were out of the blender, they were black.

But on I went. Peeling. Chopping. Grinding (and resting the overheated blender between sessions). Hours passed, but I was terrified of stopping. Oxidizing waits for no mom.

At last it was time to cook the blackened mess in a pot. It would have to be cooked, strained and cooked again until it reached a syrup stage.

So I cooked. I strained. I put it aside and got it out again the next day. The mud-colored water refused to get thick. I kept progressively smaller pots of it going on the back burner for a couple of days.

Our kids learned firsthand where sugar comes from. Right, Pete?

Finally, finally, it was syrup. And here, the instructions told me, the magic would happen. When I dropped in a few grains of store sugar, my gooey mess would seize up and become something like brown sugar.

I stood the boys on chairs around the stove and dropped in the grains.

TA DA!

Nothing.

Well, maybe it wasn't really thick enough yet. Maybe with a little more cooking time....

We all know where this is going, don't we?

It took a week for my blisters to heal. Dietitians are right: Sugar really is evil.

(Note: When I look up "mangel" and "sugar beet" today, I find them listed as different plants, with the sugar beet higher in sugar and the mangel listed as livestock feed. Could that have been the trouble all along? A simple misreading of the catalog? Maybe I should try again....)

Chapter 3:
Sizing up your site

There are several things to consider when choosing a garden site:

Sun. It takes a lot of energy to produce vegetables and fruit, so first and foremost, your garden needs at least six hours of sun exposure a day. Observe the sunlight patterns. If your plot is shaded by trees or a building, you have a choice to make.

How badly do you want that garden? Our lot was 100 percent shade when we moved in except for the narrow strip of parking by the curb. So we cut down a tree. It was a huge, cone-bearing conifer probably 70 feet tall, and a terrible decision to have to make. The ground shook when the main trunk came down.

I still feel guilty about cutting that tree. But it was the only way. We planted several replacements around the yard, but still, every time I think about it, I say a little apology to the gardening gods.

Soil. Do you live in a newer neighborhood? If so, you'll have to get right to work on the soil.

Dig down in almost any new development in Kansas City and you'll find a disheartening sight: yellowish clay. That's because all that digging and leveling of the site diminishes the black layer of loam it took centuries to create. You'll need to add topsoil and compost regularly to rebuild the soil.

Many garden experts recommend testing the soil, and then using that information to add nutrients for the best yield. And that's a fine idea, really. But it can be a little daunting for a first-timer. Unless you buy a test kit from the store, you'll have to take your sample somewhere to be tested. (Kansas and Missouri county extension offices do this for $12 to $15.) Once that's done, there is the time spent studying what to do and the expense of additives.

In all our years of gardening, we've tested the soil only once. We did not end up making any soil amendments, mainly because we couldn't afford them on such a big plot.

If you want to optimize your yields, though, a soil test and fertilizer are well worth the effort. I'd recommend having the testing done by an outside source rather than using a store test kit. The store kit we tried recently (and whose directions we followed to the letter) gave results that were unreadable.

Water and drainage. It goes without saying you should not put your garden in a low spot or, heaven forbid, in the floodplain of an active creek. Watch what happens when it rains. If water pools, this might be a site to avoid.

Buried cable. Always check before digging. Some cable isn't very deep. A schematic of the cables and pipes is always helpful. If a lot of them crisscross your land, raised beds might be the best option.

Black walnut trees. You read that right. Black walnut trees are the natural enemy of tomatoes (and peppers, potatoes and eggplants, it turns out).

For years I thought this was a tale gardeners pass on, like an urban legend. But the experts say different. Black walnuts produce a chemical called juglone that is toxic when it comes into contact with certain plants. The death zone is under the canopy of the tree, but plants also can be affected farther out depending on drainage, soil type, microorganisms and the sensitivity of the plants.

Planting near a walnut tree is like rolling the dice. You might get away with it. I've known people who say they grew tomatoes and other plants rights under a walnut. But as the garden gods giveth, so can they taketh away. The whole plant is just as likely to suddenly shrivel and die.

> # Did you know? The leaves of potatoes, rhubarb, tomatoes and eggplant are poisonous and should not be eaten. These plants, plus any other member of the nightshade family, produce solanine, which can cause intestinal distress, dizziness, headaches and—in large quantities—death. Potatoes exposed to light turn green (with chlorophyll), which can also indicate an increase in solanine.

We have a walnut along the back edge of our property, about 16 feet from the garden perimeter but 35 feet from the tomatoes. Most of the branches lean away from the garden.

So far, so good. But every year we eye it with mistrust.

Personality. What type of person are you? Look deep inside your heart. Do you start an exercise program full bore the first few weeks, then fizzle out because you overdid? Do you have problems carrying home improvement projects through to the end? If so, consider starting small with just a few plants.

Horticulturists frequently mention containers as a good option for beginners. If they are close to the house, it's even easier for new gardeners to keep a constant eye on them to see what needs attention, says Matt Bunch, horticulturist at Powell Gardens.

This pretty blossom may be a future squash.

We didn't start with containers, but we did have a very small plot. This was a good thing. We had plenty of problems with squirrels, watering, disease and pests. Multiply that times 100 square feet, and I don't know whether we'd have had the heart to continue a second year.

If, on the other hand, you are one of those people who flogs away at a project long after everyone else calls it quits, you may be ready for a bigger plot.

Just keep saying, "It will be worth it."

And it will be.

Buried potato treasure results in paltry payoff BY ROXIE

My first time growing potatoes was at a community plot in Shawnee.

I had read up on the subject and found one source that suggested great results if the newly planted spuds were covered with black plastic. The dark mulch kept potatoes that popped up from turning green, plus kept them moist and weed-free, the article said.

I went to the store, bought some potato "eyes" and a couple of rolls of black plastic and set to work.

The soil was wet and cloddy on the day I planted. When I unrolled the mulch, I caught the attention of one of my plot "neighbors."

"What's that?"

"Plastic mulch. I read you can get a lot of potatoes this way."

"You leave it on until they leaf out?"

"Oh, no," I replied confidently. "You keep it on until harvest."

Spring turned into a hot, humid summer. The potato plants poked through the holes I'd left in the mulch. Everything was going according to plan.

Every once in a while, someone ventured over from his or her own plot to ask when the mulch was coming off. They asked so often that I began to worry something was wrong.

By mid-July, it was hot. The plants had shriveled and fallen over, as potato plants are supposed to do. But being an Iowa girl, I knew potatoes could stay in the ground awhile. July seemed awfully early to dig. And we were going on a trip in a couple of days.

Sweat rolled into my eyes as I did my last weeding before the trip. One of my by-now-familiar neighbors approached with a purposeful look. Clearly, he'd been chosen to tell us something.

"So, do you figure on taking that plastic off pretty soon?"

"No, we're going on a trip. I thought I'd leave it on and let the potatoes stay in the ground," I said. We'd come out and dig them as needed through the fall.

The man had a look of shocked panic. "They'll cook! They'll cook right in the ground," he said.

After listening a minute or two, I became convinced that we would return from our trip to find a steaming, stinking pile of mush under the plastic. All that work for nothing.

I returned later with Mike and the wheelbarrow. With trepidation we tore open the plastic and started digging.

Surprise! Despite the heat and the clay clods, we turned up spadeful after spadeful of beautiful white potatoes. They were big, like the ones sold individually at grocery stores as "bakers." Truly beginners' luck. I still look back on it as our best potato year ever.

Now we had a trunk full of potatoes. But we still had to take the kids to see Grandma. What to do?

I didn't have a specific plan for keeping the potatoes. I figured we'd just dig them as needed. But now that they were out of the ground, there weren't many options. Potatoes need pressure canning, and I didn't have the equipment. We didn't have a cool dry place in the basement, or anything like a root cellar.

The only other choice I could find was to freeze them. But you can't just put a raw potato in the freezer one day and extract something edible the next. The instructions were to partly fry them first.

This took hours. The procedure is to peel the potatoes; cut them into "fries"; fry them quickly, before they turn brown, in spattery oil; and drain them. Then the oily things go into freezer bags.

It took all my time before the trip. Later that year, when the family was gathered around the dinner table eating the result of all that hard work, it was...

SO NOT WORTH IT! Worst potatoes I ever ate. Friends, do NOT try this at home.

Chapter 4:
The importance of planning

You can't get something for nothing, even in the vegetable world.

While it may seem as if you are getting those green beans and squash for free, there was a start-up cost. You bought topsoil or hoes. Seed. A roto-tiller.

So how much will a garden set you back? That depends a lot on how well you plan.

For us, January seems the natural time to start. The seed catalogs have been coming all through December. It's dreary and cold in Kansas City. Christmas is over, and the holiday bills have us dreaming of solvency.

I start by getting out my big garden binder, which has all the garden plans from years past, plus the leftover seeds. I look at the plans, take a quick inventory of what is in the freezer and the pantry and then decide how much of each vegetable we need to plant.

Keeping records, even messy ones like mine, is helpful because seed catalogs are like infomercials for miracle cleaners — very convincing. All those color pictures and promises of "super productive" vines or "luscious buttery texture" are *soooo* tempting.

But although one packet of seeds is cheap, they add up quickly. You don't want to overdo it.

My records also help me remember what did and did not work. That variety of peas that didn't produce? I'd forget it if I didn't keep a copy of my order from last year. Chances are, I'd fall for the seed catalog description a second time.

My binder contains a sketch of each year's garden plotted out in grid form. I keep the leftover seeds, still in their packets, in plastic zipper storage bags with holes punched in the margins for the binder rings. This probably isn't the perfect system, but it has worked for me for years.

Of course, you could casually decide one day to have a garden and show up at the home or garden store to buy whatever seeds and bedding plants appeal to you. That's pretty much how our first garden came about. But you will end up paying more than you have to. If you really want to save money, do the planning.

HOW MUCH SHOULD I PLANT?

If this is your first garden, you won't have the archives, but the questions are the same. What vegetables do you like and how much do you want? Do you want a few tomatoes and cucumbers for the occasional salad? Or do you have visions of a freezer full of green beans and corn?

The next issue is how much garden space you need to achieve your goal. For that, you'll need to consult your seed packets, catalog and, of course, the experience of your friends.

As your friend, let me give you a rundown:

Peas. Unless you plant an edible-pod pea (like a snow pea or a "Sugar Snap"), you will have to plant a field's worth to get enough to last through the year. Imagine a paper grocery sack filled with peas in the pod. Once shelled, you will have about a third as much. And your thumbs will be sore.

This is why many people don't plant peas. But I'm committed to them. I love the sweet green taste of new peas out of the shell and briefly simmered. In the past we've planted 80 row feet and frozen about 3 pounds of peas.

A sugar-podded pea is also a good option. If you pick them young, the pods are fat and juicy and they are good raw or lightly cooked. You can also wait until they are more mature and easier to shell and eat just the peas. The drawback is, this type can grow so tall you have to build a little fence to keep them upright.

Broccoli. If you want your broccoli to be on call for stir-fries and salads, you can get by with one or possibly two plants. You'll cut one big head early in the season and eat smaller side shoots that appear all season as the plant tries to grow new flowers.

Want a freezer full of broccoli? We've gotten about 14 pounds from 26 plants in years past.

Cauliflower and cabbage. These brassicas (members of the broccoli family) are more straightforward. You get one head per plant. Space plants 1½ to 2 feet apart.

Spinach. If spinach is a salad plant for you, you'll be fine with a few row feet. Like other plants eaten as raw leaves (lettuce, corn salad, arugula), what you see is pretty much what you get. If spinach is cut at the stem, a little may grow back before the weather turns hot.

If you want bags of frozen spinach, be prepared to commit some serious space. Spinach wilts in cooking to a fraction of its former size. And you must cook it before freezing or you'll end up with green slime.

Only in our biggest garden did we plant enough spinach to take us through the year. I don't remember how much we planted, but I'm thinking it was about 50 feet by 30 feet. I hauled it back by the garbage bag full and washed it in the bathtub. (Yes, we scrubbed and rinsed the tub before and after.) It was grueling, because spinach has to be rinsed several times to get out the grit.

Corn. The biggest space eater in any garden is sweet corn. Seeds need to be planted about a foot apart, each row about 3 feet apart and, for pollination to work, in at least four rows. If you are lucky and the critters don't find it, some short rows will give you a few meals' worth at the height of summer.

But you'll make up the money you saved in aggra-vation. Animals love corn, and they will take any risks to get it. And the taller your corn

Hot pepper: A little goes a long way.

grows, the more likely it is to be blown over by a big thunderstorm. You may find yourself out in the mud the next day, pulling it upright and desperately mounding wet soil around the roots to keep it there. We grew corn in our largest garden but gave it up a couple of years ago. (*See Garden Experiments Gone Horribly Wrong, Page 86.*)

Peppers. Don't plant more than two jalapenos or one Scotch bonnet unless you are selling them. Trust me. We love spicy food, but these peppers go into dishes at the rate of one-half to one pepper at a time. Each plant produces a lot of peppers. As a result, the bags of frozen peppers tend to pile up. I think we found one from '04 the other day. You can slice and pickle the jalapenos, but again, think of how fast you will use them.

Sweet peppers are another matter. If you want a color other than green, you must leave the pepper on the plant a long time, causing the plant to set fewer fruits than it would if you picked all green (a little economics lesson into why red and orange peppers cost so much more at the store). So it's worthwhile to put in a few extra sweet pepper plants. As a bonus, they are easy to freeze.

Potatoes. Some people don't recommend potatoes because they are usually cheap at the store. But really, there's nothing like the texture of garden potatoes, especially the marble-sized ones that go so well with new peas.

Most potatoes we plant are eaten during the summer because we haven't found a way to store them that we like. (*See Garden Experiments Gone Horribly Wrong, Page 55.*) So we are conservative on how many we plant. In the past, 20 row feet has been more than enough.

Zucchini. Someone really ought to start a program for zucchini similar to the animal welfare groups' efforts to spay and neuter dogs and cats. That way we wouldn't have to endure the heartbreak of the abandoned vegetables left on a front porch, or the pleadings of gardeners to take their little ones and please, please give them a good home.

Zucchini? We plant only one hill every second or third year. Guess what? We still have more zucchini than we want.

Winter squash. I was never a fan of winter squash until I discovered butternut squash soup. It was so good that I decided to plant four hills of Waltham butternuts. Now butternut is a family favorite. We like it because it has more squash and less seed cavity, is relatively easy to peel and keeps well without special processing. Those four hills gave us 13 good-sized squash, which we ate into February.

Cucumbers, pumpkins and vine plants. I like pickles, so I sometimes overdo it with the cucumbers. This is because our cukes are often affected by a wilt that wipes out the vines one by one. As a result, some seasons I don't get enough to pickle, and that makes me sad.

I deal with this by planting a lot in hopes that I will have plenty in case of a crop failure. One recent year I wanted a big crop, so I planted 18 hills and ended up with 13 quarts of pickles of various sorts. (I plant only "pickling" cucumbers. Picklers will work fine in salads, but salad cucumbers don't always make good pickles.)

Melons, cucumbers, squash and pumpkins take a fair amount of space because they spread by vining. You can limit the space by choosing carefully from the seed catalog. Some good summer squashes have a "bush" growing style and don't spread as much, and cucumbers can be kept in line with a small trellis. Pumpkins and other larger veggies will spread aggressively and have to be watched to keep them from taking over.

Green beans. They are one of the easiest vegetables to grow and produce a surprising amount of food. Like broccoli, they'll keep producing all summer if you keep them picked and the weather cooperates. Once we had so many green beans that I urged friends to take a cigarette lighter to the plants as they finished picking. Another year we were still picking green beans in November.

You don't need to plant a lot of beans to start, because you can add a row or two as early crops such as radishes and lettuce expire. We harvested more than 14 pounds of frozen beans from 50 row feet in 2008, which was a middling year.

Roxie's faves

Part of the fun of gardening is trying all the exciting varieties of vegetables your local grocery is too unimaginative to stock. Broccoflower, broccoli raab, Japanese eggplant, purple potatoes and tomatillos are all things we've grown because we couldn't find a reliable (and inexpensive) supply at the store.

That said, there are some varieties of mainstream vegetables we plant year after year. A short list:

Green beans. Bush Blue Lake sets on tons of straight beans with very little string. Nothing seems to bother the plants. The only year we had a failure was the dry year when spider mites destroyed them.

Sweet corn. When we grew sweet corn, it was either Honey 'N Pearl, troublesome to grow but *sooo* sweet, or Silver Queen, less sweet but a robust grower.

Spinach. The Melody hybrid has nice broad leaves.

Tomatoes. Our slicers are Celebrity, a hybrid that sets on beautiful tasty fruit.

Peas. We grew Sugar Snap for years but switched to Maestro, which had more peas per pod. Sugar Snaps have an edible pod, Maestro does not. Both are good. Also, we usually plant a short row of Oregon Sugar Pod, the flat type often used in Chinese cooking.

Butternut squash. Waltham has been a winner.

Tomatoes. Everybody's favorite. If you want tomatoes on hand only for a sandwich or a salad, one or two plants are fine. You will need to plan on enough space for the plants, plus whatever staking or caging method is used to keep them upright. The heirloom types are delicious but can be iffy producers prone to wilts. Hybrids have the advantage of disease resistance, but their seeds are more expensive and you can't save your own.

If you want to put up tomato sauce, salsa, puree or juice, paste types are a good bet. We plant 20 or so Romas every year, plus eight or nine hybrid slicers. Last year we got more than 10 gallons of puree, 2 quarts of dried, 15 pints of salsa and 2½ quarts of roasted, frozen tomato.

Warning: If you are a salad person, you may be tempted to plant a cherry tomato. If you do, make a list of friends who like cherry tomatoes, because these plants produce hundreds and hundreds of tiny fruits. In 2009, I planted a cherry tomato for the first time since the Golden Pear Tomato Jam Fiasco of '87. That was the year three plants of yellow pear tomatoes yielded quart after quart of the sweet little fruits. I dutifully made them all into preserves — which no one liked and I ended up throwing away.

Sweet potatoes. Sweet potatoes grow very well here indeed. When our sons, Sam and Pete, were little, I used to make up a bedtime story for them about how our cat hatched from a sweet potato. (The cat was the same color, and we had a few big sweet potatoes that year that were the size you might imagine a sweet-potato cat egg to be.) I always get a dozen slips from the garden catalog and interplant them with spinach. Their vines don't start taking up room until long after the spinach is gone.

Strawberries. It's great to have fresh strawberries on your cereal in the early summer. Unlike other vegetables, strawberries come back year after year with only a little maintenance. We bought plants from a garden catalog a few years ago, planted them according to the directions on the box and got a light harvest the very first year.

A dozen or fewer plants will provide berries for the summer. But since they stay over winter, it's a good idea to put strawberries in a separate bed where activities in the rest of the garden won't disturb them.

SKETCH A PLAN ON PAPER

Now it's time to get out your catalogs (or pull them up on the computer screen), graph paper and a straightedge and get busy.

Once again, consider your space. Maybe a little shade creeps into a corner part of the day. Or maybe a dreaded black walnut lurks in a neighbor's yard. No site is perfect. You'll have to adjust for that.

For us, shade and a black walnut tree are two issues we have to work around. As a result, we never plant tomatoes or sun-loving plants like peppers at the back of the garden.

Next, think about interplanting and rotation.

Some plants are natural companions. Certain herbs, like basil, and flowers, like marigolds, are good bug repellants. If you plant them close to vegetables, you reduce your chances of having to use a pesticide later. Even organic pesticides can be nasty and expensive, so you want to avoid them.

Tomato and basil are good companion plants, but there are many, many more. *Rodale's All-New Encyclopedia of Organic Gardening* (1993) has a more comprehensive list.

Crop rotation is another fine idea, practiced by the pros. Don't plant the same thing in the same place two years in a row. This keeps certain heavy feeders from depleting the soil and protects from disease, which can stay in the dirt one season to the next.

Again, there are a lot of crop rotation techniques you can check out from far better experts than us. But just keep your vegetables moving.

With that in mind, pencil in your rows and hills. If things aren't measured perfectly, you can make adjustments on the fly. I always do. The important thing is that all the brain work will be done when planting time comes and you are working against nightfall and impending rain.

Weird things we've grown BY ROXIE

Peanuts. We got goobers, though certainly not a bumper crop.

Loofah gourds. We still have one next to the bathtub.

Giant pumpkin. We had success growing a giant pumpkin the very first year we tried, but never again. Classic beginner's luck. After we carved our single success story, our youngest boy could climb inside.

Giant sunflower. It grew to be a huge, ugly eyesore. The birds ate almost all the seeds, leaving a worm-infested, empty head.

Cotton. The seed wouldn't germinate despite (or maybe because of) prolonged soaking.

Artichokes. This vegetable is biennial, meaning it bears on the second year. We grew a small plant from seed, but of course it died during the winter. There's a reason they're grown in California, apparently.

Sugar beets. See "Experiments Gone Horribly Wrong," Page 20.

Endive. The instructions called for "blanching" the plants in a protected place by piling sandy soil over them and keeping them at the correct temperature for a certain time. We ultimately decided we don't like endive that much.

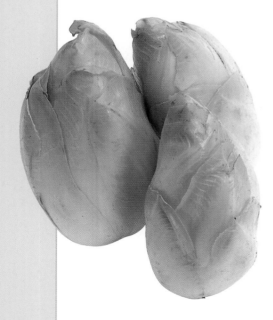

Chapter 5:
Seed starting

You have your list of vegetables. You have your garden plan. Now let the money bloodbath begin, right?

Not necessarily. If you have listened to our advice, there's still snow on the ground and lots of time. You are operating from a position of power.

At this point you have a choice: seeds or bedding plants?

Of course, bedding plants are easy and convenient. With bedding plants, you could sleep until April, then load up on plants at the nursery or home store. But listen up, slacker. If you do, we'll personally come to your house and ridicule you.

Last time I was at my favorite garden store, bedding plants were sold in 4-inch pots for $1.49 apiece. One plant per pot. If you have only 10 plants, right away you've spent $15.

But don't they sell those six-packs of the small cells for less? Yes, they do. The harried clerk I asked pointed out one table with a few sickly-looking specimens. He explained that the selection was limited.

The typical seed packet, on the other hand, costs $1.20 for common varieties to nearly $3 for fancier hybrids from upscale companies. Keep in mind that one packet may last two or three seasons.

The truth is, you can't trust that any store will have the bedding plant variety you want when you want it. And what's the point of having a garden if you don't have control over what you plant?

For us, every planting season starts not outside but in the basement. The cost of growing your own plants from seed is minimal compared with the equivalent in store-grown plants.

Not every plant has to be started as a seedling and transplanted. I go to the trouble only for broccoli, cabbage, cauliflower, peppers, tomatoes and eggplant. Once in a while, we'll put in lettuce so we can have it early. Everything else generally does fine being directly seeded into the ground once the frost danger has passed.

To set up your own basement nursery, you'll need:
- card table or other flat surface
- plastic 4-inch pots (about 40 cents apiece)
- plastic trays (about $1.50 apiece)
- small plastic markers (5 cents apiece)
- sterile soilless mix (Soilless mix, not potting soil, has always worked best for us. An 8-quart bag is about $6.50.)
- fluorescent light

About that last item. Special "grow lights" are nice, but we have found plants grow just as well with cheap fluorescent shop lights. They have to be lowered about 2 inches from the plants and then raised as the plants grow. Mike has ours hanging by wires from the basement ceiling joists.

Mike says: *I'm always worried that the cops will see the grow lights through our basement windows and think we're growing another crop down there. Then one night we'll wake up and hear our front door being kicked in by the Drug Enforcement Administration.*

Later, you may need more trays and some four- or six-packs of cells (about 15 cents apiece) into which to transplant. A heated waterproof mat (made for starting seeds) speeds along germination but is not essential. We didn't get one until our 20th year or so. They cost about $30 for the 9-by-19½-inch size.

You can use material besides plastic for seed starting. Some people like cardboard egg cartons, folded newspapers or the water-absorbing Jiffy Pellets (15 cents each). All are biodegradable. I like plastic because it is reusable. Except for the stray marker or cell, I bought these materials the first two years of gardening and have used them ever since.

THIS IS HOW YOU DO IT

It takes less time than you'd think to grow plants from seed.

Afternoon one: As soon as possible after the seeds arrive (mid-February, if you were on the ball), take them down-stairs. Wet down the soilless mix, which keeps the pots from floating when you water them later. (I'll admit skipping this step sometimes.)

Fill some 4-inch pots almost to the top. Look at your master plan to see how many plants you want and tap in that many seeds, plus a few extra just in case. Don't crowd too much because you will have to separate them later; 25 to 30 seeds is plenty.

Cover seeds lightly with more mix. Label. Put into tray. When you're done, pour about an inch of water in the tray. The water will be soaked up through the holes in the bottoms of the pots, and the seeds won't be disturbed.

Boom. You're done. If you have a heating mat, place it under the tray and turn it on. You can monkey with the lights if you want, but they aren't really needed until the first green

shoots come up. When we do turn on the lights, we put them on a timer for 18 hours a day. We find the fluorescents need a little more time than the grow lights. Keep checking on the plants and watering.

Afternoon two: Several weeks later, when your seedlings have a couple of "nor-mal" sets of leaves (not the first leaves out of the ground), you can transplant them into individual cells. Carefully loosen the plants and roots from the pots and sepa-rate as many plants as you need, plus a few extra for backup. Put them in the cells and fill in with more soilless mix. (Tomatoes and brassicas can start roots along the stem, so it's OK if some stem is submerged.)

Label as necessary. Return to the tray and water as before.

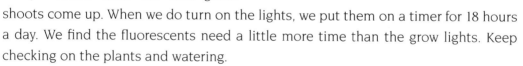

Build Mike's cold frame

Our cold frame is a no-nonsense structure that we set up in the driveway each spring and disassemble and store after our young plants have been transplanted into the garden. Essentially, it is a squat box with no bottom and a slanted lid that we prop up on warm days and close at night, or when the temperature dips on those unpredictable early spring days.

INSTRUCTIONS

1. Cut the three 2x8s in half into 4-foot lengths.
2. On one of the 4-foot pieces, draw a straight pencil line diagonally from one corner to the other. Saw along the diagonal line to form two right triangles.
3. Cut the 1x4 into five 1-foot pieces and two 9-inch pieces.
4. To assemble the back of the cold frame, lay two of the 2x8 pieces horizontally, one butted on top of the other. Join by nailing three of the foot-long 1x4s vertically across the two boards.
5. Form each side the same way, attaching a triangular piece atop a regular 4-foot section.
6. Assemble the base of the cold frame by attaching the two sides to the back with corner brackets at the top and bottom, secured with drywall screws. The remaining 4-foot board is the front. Attach it to the sides using one corner bracket per side.
7. Make the top by cutting the 2x4s in half and joining the four pieces with corner brackets. It should be about 4 inches longer than it is wide.
8. Attach lid to base with door hinges. Cut galvanized fencing to fit the top of the lid and staple.
9. Drape plastic sheeting over top so a few inches hang over the sides. Cut to fit and secure to sides of lid by nailing furring strips or window molding over the plastic. Make sure the sheeting stays taut.
10. Attach the stake that props up the lid by drilling a ½-inch hole into the center of the front of the lid. Drill another ½-inch hole through a 4-foot piece of treated 1x2. Secure loosely with carriage bolt, nut and washer.

MATERIALS

3 (8-foot) pieces pressure-treated
    2x8s
1 (8-foot) piece pressure-treated 1x4
2 heavy-duty door hinges
2 (8-foot) pieces pressure-treated
    2x4s
3 (8-foot) lengths 1x2 furring strips
 Small roll 4-mill plastic sheeting
Galvanized fencing measuring
    4 x 4 feet
Drywall screws
Nails
10 galvanized 3-inch corner brackets
1 4 x $^3/_8$-inch carriage bolt
1 flat washer
1 nut

TOOLS YOU'LL NEED

Circular saw
Electric drill
Claw hammer
Screwdriver

If you have a small garden, the second afternoon is not strictly necessary. You can divide the plants out of the pots and put them straight into the garden. Transplanting gives them extra growing room.

From here on out, the biggest challenge is remembering to check the water levels. Both afternoons should have taken no more than a couple of hours.

At this point you are home free until about a week before planting time. Then you'll need to put the seedlings outside at least part of the time to toughen them.

Watch the weather reports. When it gets to be early April and nighttime temperatures consistently stay above freezing, we put our seedlings in the portable cold frame that Mike built. (*See instructions on Page 44.*)

A cold frame is a small structure that lets in sunlight and protects plants from harsh wind and cold. If you don't have a cold frame, put the seedlings in a spot protected from wind for a week or so. But keep watching the nighttime lows. You're not really safe until mid- to late May.

Afternoon three: Plant your seedlings in their new home. Measure with a planting stick (*see instructions on Page 47*), dig a hole with a trowel, insert plant and fill in with soil. For extra protection from cutworms, which will clip off tender plants at the stem, we put a couple of small sticks in the ground close to the stems. It seems to work.

Water each plant. We usually cover them for a week with clean, uncapped plastic jugs (milk or cooking oil) whose bottoms have been sawed off. When anchored to the ground with mud so they won't blow away, the jugs act like mini greenhouses, with air circulating through the open tops. This way we're covered if it gets close to freezing. We do this even when it's warm to protect young plants from wind damage.

The broccoli family, which includes, cabbage, cauliflower, kohlrabi, kale and turnips, can handle the cool nights of early April. Tomatoes seem to do better if you wait until the middle of the month to plant them.

DIRECT SEEDING

It's even easier to plant seeds straight into the garden. Get a hoe, your seeds, your garden plan and measuring device. Mark the designated spot with stakes. Make a fur-

Did you know?

Some seeds should be soaked a few hours before planting to help them germinate. Soaking especially helps beets, spinach, corn and peas.

Make Mike's planting stick BY MIKE

You needn't beg, borrow, steal or (worst case) buy all your garden tools. Sometimes you can make them. That's how we came to own a planting stick.

Never heard of one? It's like a yardstick, only it is heavy-duty and made for people like us, who figure only three numbers are necessary in the garden.

Six, six and six, as in inches, rather than the sign of the Beast.

To make spacing between rows simple and easy, Roxie uses a 4-foot measuring stick I ingeniously designed by marking it off with green paint at 6-inch intervals.

"It's simple," Roxie says. "I don't need to read any numbers. I know how long it is at a glance."

We leave grow lights on about 18 hours a day.

row and plant according to the spacings listed on the seed packet. Rule of thumb: The bigger the seeds, the farther apart they should be planted and the more dirt is needed to cover them.

Most vegetables are planted in rows, but melon and cucumber vines branch out in all directions. Plant them by grouping two or three seeds in the soil every few feet. You can hill the dirt up around the area. Or not.

Not everything should be planted from seed. Potatoes come to mind, as do onions, shallots and garlic.

We tried onions from seed once and…uh…yeah. Save yourself some pain and buy sets or bulbs from the garden store. They are just as cheap and much, much easier. (With onions, do try to look as you plant and place the root side down, pointy side up. But if you mess up, they'll grow anyway.)

I've never even seen potato seed offered. Potatoes sprout from "eyes," which are the things that sprout if you leave them too long on the shelf. If you buy seed potatoes, cut them into pieces, with an eye on each piece, and let them air-dry until the

Did you know? Potatoes and garlic from the grocery store can be planted in the garden. You won't get the same guarantee of disease resistance you might get from certified seed stock, though.

cut sides seal over. Or you can spend extra and buy potato "eyes" that have already been cut and cured.

The easiest way, though, is to shop for the smallest seed potatoes possible and not cut them at all. It is worth it to avoid the aggravation.

(Note: Grocery store potatoes and garlic will work, although some have been treated to slow sprouting. Once I saw purple potatoes at the store that were seriously sprouted and decided to try them in the garden. "Let me see if there are some better ones in back," the checkout lady said. No, thanks, I'll be happy to take these. And they ended up being free.)

Did you know?
You don't have to order fresh seeds every year. Most seeds can be saved a couple of years if they are kept dry and safe from temperature extremes, although germination rates decline as seeds age. Date the seed packets so you know how old they are.

WATCH THE WEATHER

Yes, planting is easy. But that doesn't mean you can do it without thinking. If you want to be successful, you have to plant in stages, according to what each plant needs.

The timing is dictated by the first and last average frost dates for the area. We'll mention them here, but beware: This is an inexact prediction. We've found that it is best to know the average dates, then watch what each particular year looks like.

In Kansas City, the last time in spring you can expect frost is mid- to late April. There is a 50 percent chance the last frost will occur by April 7 and a 90 percent chance it will happen by April 21, according to the National Oceanic and Atmospheric Administration.

As for the first frost, there's a 10 percent likelihood it will happen by Oct. 14 and a 50 percent likelihood by Oct. 28. The growing season is the time between the last and first frosts.

Some plants grow well only in cool weather, while others won't come up until the soil is warm. For simplicity, I've put them into groups:

The earlies. Lettuce, radishes, peas, onions, potatoes, spinach, cauliflower, cabbage and broccoli. All except maybe the lettuce and spinach can handle a little light

49

frost or even a late snow.

The lates. Carrots, beets, beans and tomatoes (with protection). No frost, please, but a few cool nights are OK.

The super-lates. Melons, corn, squash, sweet potatoes and basil.

For more detailed information, see the chart (opposite) from our friends at K-State Research and Extension.

No, we're not dairy farmers. Plastic milk jugs keep young plants warm and protect them from the wind.

Vegetable Planting Calendar

Legend: Plant (light) · Harvest (dark)

	MARCH	APRIL	MAY	JUNE	JULY	AUG.	SEPT.	OCT.	NOV.
Beans (Lima)			Plant			Beans (Lima–Bush) Harvest			
Beans (Lima)			Plant				Beans (Lima–Pole) Harvest		
Beans (Snap)			Plant	Beans (Snap) Harvest					
Beans (Snap)					Plant		Beans (Snap) Harvest		
Beets	Plant			Beets Harvest	Plant			Beets Harvest	
Broccoli	Plant			Broccoli Harvest		Plant		Broccoli Harvest	
Cabbage	Plant			Cabbage Harvest		Plant		Cabbage Harvest	
Carrots		Plant		Carrots Harvest	Plant			Carrots Harvest	
Cauliflower	Plant			Cauliflower Harvest	Plant			Cauliflower Harvest	
Chard		Plant		Chard Harvest					
Collards		Plant	Collards Harvest						
Cucumbers			Plant		Cucumbers Harvest				
Eggplant			Plant			Eggplant Harvest			
Endive	Plant			Endive Harvest	Plant			Endive Harvest	
Kale						Plant		Kale Harvest	
Lettuce	Plant		Lettuce Harvest						
Lettuce		Plant	Lettuce Harvest						
Lettuce							Plant	Lettuce Harvest	
Melons			Plant			Melons Harvest			
Okra			Plant		Okra Harvest				
Onions	Plant					Onions Harvest			
Onion Sets / Green Onions		Plant	Green Onions Harvest						
Peas	Plant			Peas Harvest					
Peppers			Plant			Peppers Harvest			
Potatoes	Plant			Potatoes Harvest	Plant			Potatoes Harvest	
Pumpkins			Plant				Pumpkins Harvest		
Radish	Plant	Radish Harvest					Plant	Radish Harvest	
Salsify		Plant					Salsify Harvest		
Spinach	Plant	Spinach Harvest					Plant	Spinach Harvest	
Squash / W. Squash		Plant / W. Squash			Squash Harvest		Winter Squash Harvest		
Sweet Corn		Plant			Sweet Corn Harvest				
Sweet Potatoes			Plant				Sweet Potatoes Harvest		
Tomatoes		Plant			Tomatoes Harvest				
Turnips	Plant		Turnips Harvest			Plant		Turnips Harvest	

Source: Charles Marr, "Vegetable Garden Planting Guide," Kansas State University (1992).

Chapter 6:
DIY tomato cages

If you grow tomatoes in the ground rather than in one of those goofy upside-down tomato hangers, you have two choices to keep them upright: Tie them to a pole or cage them. Most people opt for cages because it's easier. Yet I smirk at the sight of those spindly, puny tomato cages sold in most stores.

The pitiful things would topple under the weight of the brawny plants growing in our garden. Or the welds would fail. Soon they would end up in the garbage.

You can buy sturdier cages, but at a premium price. Fifteen dollars for one cage? Not in my budget.

That's why I suggest building your own cages. There are any number of do-it-yourself versions on the Internet, from wooden cages to cages made of plastic pipe.

With as many tomato plants as we grow, I needed a quick and easy way to make sturdy cages that were inexpensive and would last a lifetime.

HERE'S MY METHOD:

• Buy a roll of galvanized steel farm fencing of whatever length you think you'll use. It comes in various heights. The type I use is 38 inches tall and divided into 6-inch squares.

You can make cages with 4-inch or smaller mesh that look more attractive. But the advantage of the 6-inch square is that you can reach in to harvest your tomatoes, whereas the others have you harvesting from the top.

• With wire cutters, snip the fencing into 5-foot sections. Form each section into a cylinder, and then wire together by twisting the cut ends together.

• Place the cage over young plants and anchor it to the ground with tent stakes. Or do as I do and thread rebar, a metal pipe or a wooden tomato stake through the weave and pound into the ground.

It's a good idea to buy more fence than you'll need. Whatever is left over from making the cages can be cut into lengths for cucumber vines and peas to climb on.

I also roll some out each fall to corral my leaves until there's room for them in the composter.

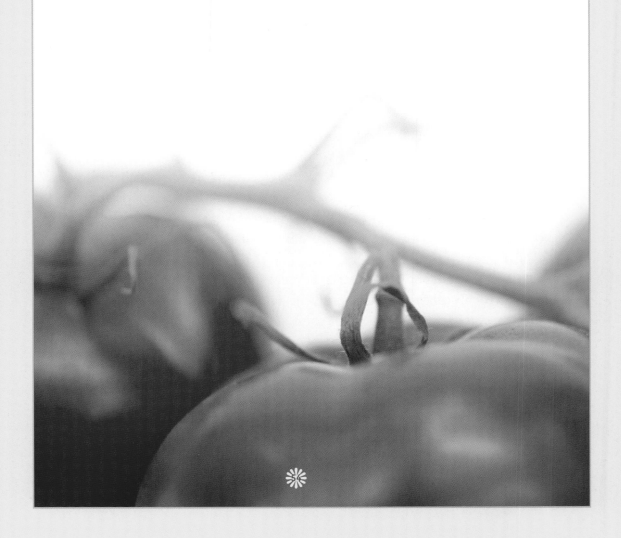

Spuds do the backstroke in underground storage tank BY ROXIE

The second year I grew potatoes, I had past success under my belt and was confident I could grow enough to feed us for a year. If only we had a way to keep them.

Never again would I par-fry and freeze potatoes. No. This year, I had a plan.

I had done some research on potato storage. Root cellars were the most recommended method, but we didn't have the room or the resources. However, I found instructions for the next best thing. You dig a hole, put the potatoes in a garbage can lined with straw and put the can in the hole.

Brilliant. The soil keeps the temperature low enough to preserve the potatoes without freezing them. The straw keeps them from rotting. The garbage can keeps out the varmints. What could go wrong?

I explained the whole thing to Mike, whom I find to be generally willing to do the muscle work behind my schemes, especially if it involves saving money.

We bought a shiny new garbage can and decided on a spot out back. Checked for cables. Then Mike got the spade and I watched him go.

Down, down, down. Garbage can depth. Then deeper, to leave room for the exterior straw lining. Deeper still, to make sure the top was submerged. At last we had our pseudo root cellar.

It was, again, a bumper year for potatoes. We filled that garbage can with potatoes and straw — gloating a little about our superior intelligence — then went on to other things, secure in the knowledge that the Hendricks household would never endure the potato famine of my ancestors.

A few weeks later, I decided to have spuds for supper. I put on my raincoat and went to retrieve my golden prize.

Uh...Mike, come out here.

The garbage can bobbed happily inside its hole, which was completely filled with muddy water and straw. And the potatoes? Was it too much to ask that the potatoes stayed dry?

Yes, it was.

Come spring we filled the hole and never spoke of it again.

Chapter 7:
Weeding & watering

My favorite part of vegetable growing—aside from eating all that "free" food in winter—is the daily walk.

It is pretty much what it sounds like. I go out to the patch, take off my shoes (or not) and walk around and look at things. Some gardening pros say looking at and getting to know your plants is the most important thing you can do to keep a vegetable garden healthy. They say you need to see how the plants grow on a daily basis to know when something is wrong and needs attention.

That's all well and good and practical. But here's why I like the daily walk: It gives me ample time for gloating, self-congratulation and daydreaming.

Look at those tomatoes! One good rain and a couple of warm days and they just took off! Grocery store tomatoes — pah! People don't know what they're missing. At least my family knows what good food is supposed to taste like. Mike is so lucky he married me. Look at how many baby butternuts are coming on. Some people will pay $1.60 a pound for winter squash at the store. Idiots. I'm too…what's that interesting pattern on this leaf? Look how the little bumps line up with such perfect spacing. Wh…uh-oh.

And then it's off to the Internet or a gardening book to figure out what kind of bug those eggs belong to. That is, if I didn't smash them on the spot.

More often than not, I'm close up and peering into the plants, gleefully counting my future peppers or green beans, when I see these problems. So, really, if it weren't for the gloating, our garden would not be nearly as good. Maybe this chapter's best

Opposite: The daily walk is the time to get acquainted with your plants.

advice should be: "Develop serious egomania."

For most of the summer, garden problems fall into three main categories: weeding, watering and pests.

WEEDING

This seems like a no-brainer, right? You see a weed; you pull it. End of story.

It is possible, though, to mess up this seemingly simple aspect of gardening.

Here are a few of our weeding mistakes from years gone by. Learn from them.

Mistake #1: "It's too muddy to weed."

No, it's not. It's just right. Nevertheless, it took us awhile to realize that getting yourself covered head-to-toe is worth it if it means you can pull — easily — those nasty, long-rooted, nutrient-sucking weeds all the way out of the ground. Yes, you can get them with the hoe, but if you wait for the ground to dry, they'll have time to get bigger, which brings us to

Mistake #2: "I'll get them when I have time."

You have time. Now. Baby nettles are easily pulled by hand. But if you wait too long, you will be stung with their stickers and sorry, so sorry. Lambsquarter and amaranth will become the size of small trees if left too long. You'll need a machete. And the grasses! Don't even think about letting them go.

Mistake #3: "I've pulled them out of the soil. They must be dead now."

Listen carefully. They aren't necessarily dead. It's just a ruse. If you pull them, leave their carcasses between rows and then, say, step on them as you go about your work, you are in for a surprise. Parts of those weeds can quickly sprout again where they touch the soil, particularly if it stays wet. You didn't pull them; you transplanted them.

Purslane, in particular, is a Plant That Will Not Die. You can leave piles of it stacked along the edge of the garden and it will stay green for days. The horror! (But on the other hand, some say it's delicious.)

Mistake #4: "Oh, well, at least they're compost."

Stop right there. Do not compost the weeds, especially if they have seeds. If you do, you're just planting them in next year's garden. Hello, Mr. Chickweed? May I help you starve my vegetables and give me a backache?

Chris Conatser

BY ROXIE

EXPERT FORAGER TOUTS THE INCREDIBLE, EDIBLE WEED

Weeds seem so robust; garden vegetables, by comparison, so puny and frail. Why is it we spend so much time cultivating the stubborn lettuce when it would be so much easier to eat the weeds?

Maybe we should, says Chris Conatser, who has made a lifelong study of the subject.

"I've always been interested in things that grow without much effort on our part. Maybe it would make a little more sense to make use of what's already there," says Conatser, who gathers wild edibles for the Justus Drugstore restaurant in Smithville, Mo., and formerly oversaw landscaping at Powell Gardens.

Chris Conatser

Many of the plants we know as weeds are not only edible but also delicious and nutritious, he says. (Common purslane has been cited as a source of omega-3 fatty acids and antioxidants.) Some were used for years by our ancestors but fell out of favor as we gravitated to traditional garden crops.

We caught up with Conatser at the Kansas City Community Gardens near Swope Park. Within seconds of setting foot in the open spaces between garden plots, Conatser had identified, picked and urged us to sample several edible weeds. Shepherd's purse had tiny, peppery seeds tucked inside flat, pale-yellow pods. Wood sorrel's elongated pods exploded in sourness as we tasted them. Pineapple weed smelled like its namesake and makes an excellent tea, he said, and dandelions have a bitterness that must be mitigated by a long cooking time and seasoning.

Other edibles we saw: Young plantain leaves, tiny purplish henbit flowers, amaranth and purple clover. Even nettles and cattail shoots are edible if they are picked young, he said. But we didn't see any that day.

Conatser has two cautions for anyone planning to forage wild plants: Don't forage if you don't know whether the area has been sprayed, and be absolutely sure you know what you are eating.

MULCH HELPS KEEP WEEDS AT BAY

Yes, Rox, regular weeding is important, essential, the mark of a responsible gardener. However, as the guy who pulls, hoes and disposes of most of the weeds that take root in our garden, my philosophy is this:

If there is any way weeding can be avoided entirely, or the frequency reduced to almost never, and still have a weed-free garden, then by all means, let's go for it.

That's why I go for mulch.

Count me as a huge fan of this environmentally friendly organic substance that frees me of mind-numbing labor.

A couple-inches-thick layer of grass clippings, straw or other mulching material spread around your plants keeps the weeds at bay. Mulch denies weeds the light and air that virtually every plant needs to survive.

The weeds that do poke through the mulch layer are easily pulled. That's because the soil under the mulch tends to stay moist and pliable longer than soil that's been exposed to the sun and wind. That "thin hard crust," as Steinbeck described the drought-packed ground of Dust Bowl Oklahoma in *The Grapes of Wrath*, is also an apt description of Kansas City soils about mid-August.

What? You didn't expect references to fine literature in a garden book?

Our dirt gets hard and dry as plywood under the punishing sun. And that's the other reason, besides weed control, that experienced gardeners apply mulch. It reduces the need for watering.

That's good for your budget as well as your back. The gardener who fails to apply mulch is the gardener who enjoys paying high water bills.

You can buy mulch, of course. But my low-cost strategy is to mulch our garden with grass clippings, which are free.

After mowing, I dump garbage cans full of clippings into the garden rows and spread them around the plants, being careful not to crowd plant stalks and stems, which might encourage rot.

I start in spring, when the soil is moist and the clippings plentiful. I'll continue to spread them in the garden until late August. By September, I'm tired and done battling the weeds. After all, the October freeze will take care of whatever weeds get past me.

If you apply a lot of chemicals to your yard (really, you shouldn't), I think it's best

to wait a few days after an application of weed killer to mow and collect clippings.

Some gardners buy mulch. We gather it in a grass catcher.

I could be wrong. Chelsey Wasem, a horticulturist at K-State Research and Extension in Johnson County, says clippings from chemically treated grass pose little risk to garden plants. Still, why take the chance?

Wasem and other experts say it's also best to avoid laying down wet clippings, as this can encourage fungus. So mow in the afternoon or evening rather than the morning, when the blades of grass are heavy with dew.

Chopped leaves are another great mulching material that you can store in the fall and apply in spring and summer. Instead of raking your leaves in autumn, run over them with a power mower. Use a bagger or rake up the excess. Any leaf fragments left over make good fertilizer for your lawn.

I don't recommend bags of cypress mulch, wood bark, etc., from the hardware store. Besides being needlessly expensive, wood mulch is a mess to clean up and can result in the occasional splinter.

And I like to garden in my bare feet whenever possible.

Of course, other gardeners have their own mulching techniques. Our friend Ron in Old Town Lenexa spreads a layer of straw atop a layer of grass clippings. Other gardeners extol the advantages of starting with a layer of cardboard or newspaper (stacked eight sheets thick).

All the above materials have the advantage of being biodegradable — just till the mulch into the soil at the end of the season. They are also free or relatively inexpensive.

Of course, you can always use a shortcut method: Buy landscape fabric or black plastic sheeting. This can cost some dough if you have a large garden plot. And why spend money to achieve a goal that can be met without opening your wallet?

WATERING

For nearly a decade, we tended a large garden lot that had gone to weeds and belonged to the neighbor lady down the street.

Her husband, the gardener, had passed on. The plot was about 6,000 square feet of tilled, black dirt.

With all that room we could grow 75 tomato plants, two stands of sweet corn, peppers, broccoli, lettuce, etc. — and so many pumpkins that our hands grew sore from carving jack-o'-lanterns. One Halloween, our kids had two dozen carved pumpkins lined up along the front porch.

But there was one huge disadvantage to that garden: We had no ready access to water. Plants need water. Yet here we were, dryland farmers in a dry land.

Occasionally I'd pass a $20 bill to the landowner in exchange for access to the water spigot at the house next door.

But mostly we depended on the kindness of Mother Nature. We mulched like crazy to preserve what moisture the ground held for as long as possible.

Nowadays, Roxie and I are fortunate enough to have a smaller but very nice-sized garden on our own property. We water whenever we want.

Still, we like to avoid paying high water bills. There aren't enough rain barrels in Lenexa to suit our needs, although we highly recommend rain barrels for people who plant in containers or smaller, raised beds.

Except during times of punishing drought, we might water our garden just a few times a year:

• We water in spring, when seeds are sown or seedlings are transplanted into the

Thanks to Sam, young seedlings get a drink.

garden, and then we water plants individually so as not to encourage weed growth in the bare patches. We give just enough water to get the plants going, and then we pray for regular rain.

• We water when plants show signs of stress — curled leaves or fruit that's obviously stunted because of lack of moisture.

• We water when we think certain crops could use a boost, especially those that are setting on fruit when the weather won't cooperate. For example, tomatoes, corn, peas and beans.

Other times, we let nature take care of it. We believe plants often adapt to the rhythms of Mother Nature.

Be aware that overwatering poses its own problems. Tomatoes that get too much water don't have that rich flavor. And a water surplus can cause the roots to stay shallow. The year most of the Midwest got flooding was also the year our tomatoes flopped over because of shallow roots.

HOW TO WATER
Turf experts recommend an inch of rain a week to keep lawns green and lush. Gardens aren't like that. Some plants like lots of water — lettuce and spinach, for

instance. Others — beets, broccoli, pepper, garlic and carrots — are happy with less. All plants prefer a good soaking rather than a daily spritzing that wets the topsoil, evaporates quickly and fails to reach the roots.

Though time-consuming, I advocate watering plants individually whenever possible. A good tool is a watering wand, the kind with a shower-like head that diffuses the water pressure and gives each plant a good soaking. That way you don't pound the plants to death by setting the hose on them.

If your schedule allows, water in the morning or early evening, when the soil is cooler and there is less evaporation. Midday watering is wasteful (evaporation again) and not as effective. Don't water late at night, because wet leaves can lead to fungus and attract slugs.

As Roxie says, it is essential to tour the garden every day. Take a good look to see which plants are thirsty and which aren't.

HOSES AND SPRINKLERS

When I think the entire garden could use a drink — and if I'm feeling particularly lazy — I drag out the sprinkler and soak the plants for a couple of hours.

I have used rotary sprinklers on occasion, both the small, cheap types and the pricey, heavy-duty kinds that look like tractors. Rotary sprinklers work fine. But they also tend to pelt your crops if they are not set correctly.

That is why I prefer an oscillating sprinkler that gently rains water down on your garden. If you don't have one, spend the extra money for the ones made out of metal. The plastic ones are junk, and you'll end up replacing them after a season or two.

Soaker hoses are more economical and waste less water because water oozes at ground level, close to the roots, rather than spraying from above. You water only the plant rows, skipping the bare patches. But they are more work to move around. So it's a balancing act: labor vs. conservation vs. expense.

Compost Happens BY MIKE

We're blessed to live on a half-acre lot studded with big shade trees.

Well, to us it's a blessing. Others might see bagging all those leaves as a curse.

In fact, it's no problem. We never leave leaf bags for the trash guys to pick up after fall or spring cleanup. We toss all those leaves in the compost pile — except for the ones that blow down the street to who knows where. (OK, I sometimes help send them on their way.)

Leaves, grass clippings, garden refuse, coffee grounds, eggshells and other kitchen scraps (no meat or grease) all wind up in the composter.

Remember, I'm lazy. So I don't turn my compost as often as some do. But my twice-a-year routine still produces a rich, black amalgam I spread over the garden each fall. Then, with my roto-tiller, I incorporate it into the soil along with any composted horse manure we've been lucky enough to acquire. I use no other fertilizer.

Compost adds nutrients to your soil, while loosening the texture so water and air can circulate.

If you want to know more about composting, the Missouri and K-State extension services have excellent publications. Find them on the Web at extension.missouri.edu or at www.oznet.k-state.edu.

It's possible to make compost without an enclosure. Simply start a pile in a corner of the yard. You can also buy a plastic composter at a store, online or through garden catalogs. But they can be pricey.

Another option is to build your own composter out of concrete blocks or treated lumber. Missouri extension provides instructions on a block composter.

I built my two-stage wooden composter based on instructions from that gardening bible of the 1980s, *The New Victory Garden* by the late Bob Thomson. I say based, because Bob's instructions shorted you on the lumber and required more bolts than I thought necessary. *(See instructions on Pages 66 and 67.)*

The composter has two separate bins so that the organic material can be turned after it's "cooked" for a while. As fresh organic material decays, use a pitchfork to move the contents of one composting bin to the other. Air and moisture will turn garden refuse into rich soil that your plants will love. Occasionally turning your compost speeds up the process.

Build Mike's composter

A small investment of time and materials will pay off in lots of compost (aka "black gold") for the garden. No turning is needed with a two-bin composter like this one.

MATERIALS

12 pieces pressure-treated 2x4, each 8 feet long

20 linear feet 4-foot galvanized wire fence, 2-by-4- inch mesh or smaller

Handful 3-inch nails

¾-inch galvanized staples

6 (³/₈-by 6-inch) carriage bolts

4 (4-inch) carriage bolts

10 (³/₈-inch) nuts

TOOLS YOU'LL NEED

Circular or hand saw

Claw hammer

Wire cutters

Heavy- duty staple gun

Electric drill

³/₈-inch wrench or socket (crescent-style wrench will do)

INSTRUCTIONS

1. Cut eight 2x4s in half so you have 16 identical 4-foot-long pieces.
2. Use 12 of those pieces to make three identical 4-foot-square panels. Nail the sections together.
3. Build a 4-by-8-foot panel using two of the 8-foot pieces and three of the 4-foot pieces, one for either end and one for a center support.
4. Cut fencing to size with wire cutters and staple to one side of each of the four panels.
5. Attach the three smaller sections to the larger one by drilling holes with a wood bit and inserting the 6-inch bolts. Tighten nuts. If you were looking at the structure from above, it would look like an "E."
6. Nail one of the remaining 8-foot pieces of lumber to the bottom of the bin's front to provide stability.
7. Lay the remaining 8-foot 2x4 over the top of the front of the composter. At its center, where it lies atop the middle 4x4 foot section, cut it on the diagonal. Attach these two stabilizing pieces at each end and in the center by drilling holes and inserting the 4-inch carriage bolts. Swing out or remove these pieces when turning the compost.

Chapter 8:
Thinning & pruning

You've planted, pulled weeds, watered when necessary. You look at your garden every day, and the plants seem to be on their way.

Really, there isn't a lot more to do. Just one or two more things. (You knew it was coming, didn't you?)

THINNING

In an ideal world, each seed would be planted exactly as far as it needs to be from its neighbor, and every seed would germinate, no exceptions. Then there would be no need for thinning.

Thinning is the most heartbreaking chore in the garden because it involves pulling out extra seedlings, undoing the work you've done. Yes, you are killing the babies.

It's necessary, though, because in the real world, it's not possible to control exactly how the seeds, especially those tiny ones, fall in the rows. If you keep seeds for a couple of years, you can't always be sure how many will sprout. If you have extras and don't thin, the plants will end up crowding one another and none will do as well as it could have.

Sometimes you can eat the fruits of your thinning (baby beets, baby lettuce), and that softens the pain. But sometimes you can't.

I usually start with stern intentions to thin to exactly the right spacing (which you should get from your seed packet) but then get too emotional to do the job quite right.

Just a little closer won't do any harm, will it? OK, so I'll put up with somewhat smaller spinach this year.

BLANCHING

If you grow cauliflower, you need to know that it's a little…uh…special. It needs to be tied up.

There's a name for this. It's called "blanching." (What did you think I was going to say?)

Blanching means that you keep light away from a part of the plant that needs to be light-colored or, in the case of cauliflower, white. Other vegetables that sometimes are blanched include asparagus and endive. But since we don't usually blanch those, I'll mention only the cauliflower technique here.

To blanch cauliflower, watch for the first sign of a head developing in the center of the plant. When you see one, pull the big leaves from the sides together in the middle and tie with twine. This keeps sunlight from turning the cauliflower head an ugly (but still edible) yellow.

By the way, some catalogs advertise certain varieties as "self-blanching." Don't believe it. Every single one of these I've grown over the years turned yellow if I didn't tie.

PRUNING

Depending on how your tomatoes are propped up, they may need to be pruned. If they are tied to single stakes, you will need to train them by cutting back side shoots until you have one main trunk.

Some people swear by this but, honestly, I never had enough time to train my kids and train my dog, let alone train my tomatoes. Instead, Mike puts a wire corral around each one and we let them grow with the fencing holding up the branches. (*See Chapter* 6, DIY *tomato cages, Page* 53.)

We don't bother with pruning anything else. We occasionally turn a pumpkin vine to stop it from attacking a pepper plant or from running amok in the yard. Otherwise, the growing is pretty much up to the plants.

PICKING

Picking is pretty intuitive. A few exceptions:

Leafy greens. You can pull these by the roots, but that would be a waste. Most plants whose leaves are eaten, including basil, will grow more if you pull off at the leaf instead. Of course, you can do this only so long before the plant bolts.

No, the lettuce doesn't run away screaming when it sees you coming. Bolting is what happens to early spring plants once the weather turns warm. Seemingly in seconds, spinach, lettuce and radishes grow a central spire that flowers and seeds if left that long. Once this happens, the leaves or roots become bitter and unusable.

Signs a plant is about to bolt: The leaves stand up taller and may change to a pointier shape. You might see longer stems on the leaves, particularly in the middle.

If you want white cauliflower, you'll have to shield it from the sun.

Potatoes, sweet potatoes, onions, garlic. Sweet potatoes should be dug before frost, while the vines look green, healthy and upright. Dig white and golden potatoes in mid-July or later, after the green plant falls over (unless you want "baby" size).

If you plan to store these vegetables any length of time, you'll first need to cure them by letting them spend a little time out of the soil.

For onions, garlic and shallots, curing allows the skins to dry and become papery. It also gives potatoes a chance to form a seal over the little cuts they got when you nicked them with the digging fork.

Our curing method: Staple chicken wire or dog wire with 2-by-4-inch mesh atop a frame of 1x2s. Lay newspapers under the frames and set the vegetables on top of

A word about herbs BY ROXIE

Herbs are among the easiest of all garden plants to grow. We plant annual herbs (the kind that die off each winter) with our vegetables because they are delicious and can deter bugs.

Annual herbs such as basil, dill and cilantro are the nice herbs, the obedient herbs. They stay pretty much where you plant them.

Chances are you may want more than these three herbs to flavor your cooking. In that case, here's some advice about planting perennials (a plant that may go dormant in winter and come up again in spring):

Find a sunny spot far away from your vegetable garden. Is it far enough away? We doubt it. Go even farther.

Now dig a moat around the outside of the patch and fill it with water. Do you have mint in your perennial patch? Then pour oil on the water and set it ablaze.

With luck, your vegetable patch may now be safe from invasion by the herbs.

Of course, we're kidding about the moat and fire, but barely. Perennial herbs can be persistent and aggressive, especially mint, horseradish and lemon verbena. Bugs don't seem to bother them. Harsh weather doesn't faze them. But watch out if you change your mind. Once planted, it's hard to get rid of them.

They spread by seeds and sometimes through a strong root system. Horseradish, for instance, has a deep root growing downward. If you plant too much—let's say three plants, just to name a figure—you might try to get rid of them by pulling them. But if you break any of that root, the broken parts will stay in the ground and grow new plants. (Hey, kids! Just like the broom on "The Sorcerer's Apprentice"!)

Chives, sage, rosemary, tarragon, oregano, marjoram, bay, lemon grass, thyme and mint (in isolation on the far side of the driveway) fill almost all our perennial herb needs.

These herbs are the one exception to my rule

Cilantro (opposite) and dill.

against bedding plants. For perennial herbs, I heartily recommend buying a small pot from the garden store. Most of these herbs have seeds the size of dust and are tricky to germinate. (Rule of thumb: If the seed packet contains another, tiny packet inside, I don't mess with it.)

Another recommendation: Put the herb garden close to the kitchen door. That way you can sneak out in your bathrobe if you want chives on those scrambled eggs.

In the fall we pot up the rosemary, thyme, marjoram, bay and lemon grass and bring them inside for the winter. Otherwise they don't need much tending. Just make sure there's enough water, and they're all but trouble-free.

After picking, onions must be cured to allow the skins to dry.

the wire. There should be room below and between the vegetables for air to circulate.

We cure veggies on the front porch, where they are protected from rain and sunlight. (Potatoes will turn green in too much light.) It's also a good idea to pick off the dirt, as it holds moisture. We don't rinse, though, to avoid waterlogging.

When the onion, garlic and shallot skins look papery and dry after at least a week, they're ready. The potatoes may be done a little sooner. Then we move our cured crops to the basement, spreading the potatoes on a table and hanging the onions and garlic in the plastic mesh bags that grocery onions come in. Nothing goes in the refrigerator, though we eventually peel and chop shallots and store them in the freezer.

Broccoli. How much is it worth to you to impress your friends with big, gorgeous broccoli heads in late June? What if I said you could also get second heads a few weeks later only a little smaller than the first? Now how much?

But wait! There's more! You can get the bigger heads, plus the slightly smaller second heads and little shoots perfect for salads or stir-fries all through the summer! Impossible, you say?

But true. All you have to do is give in to the impulse to be lazy.

Once you cut that first broccoli, leave the headless plants in the garden. They will continue to sprout side shoots as long as you continue to pick. On occasion, when the weather has been just right, the first side shoots have been almost as big as the original head. The sprouting stops when flowers and seeds form.

Therein lies a universal truth about the harvesting of all vegetables. They won't hold forever. You can't ask your family to go out and pick them and accept this answer: "Oh, when I get around to it. I should have time at the end of the week."

Picture every green bean, potato and eggplant with a tiny clock on it. Every minute past its prime, that vegetable gets drier and tougher. You have to keep picking, even if you don't need peppers that day. Otherwise, nature will tell the plant it already has enough maturing seeds to have done its reproductive duty. At that point, it will stop setting on new fruit and there won't be any next week, when you really wanted that vegetarian pot pie.

ADVANCED TECHNIQUES—THE FALL GARDEN

I call this "advanced" because it is somewhat tricky to get new crops growing in the middle of the summer and ready before first frost. Things have to be timed just right, and plants have to be watched and nursed more than in the spring.

Some plants (sweet potatoes, peppers) take too long to grow a second crop in Kansas City. Shorter-season crops, though, can be planted a second time in a vacant area. If you are smart, careful and very, very lucky, you will get something for your trouble.

First, it helps to know when to plant your second crop. I recommend the vegetable garden calendar printed by K-State Research and Extension (*see Page* 51). This handy chart lists planting and harvest times for most vegetables it's feasible to grow here.

Next, decide what to plant. I've had the most success with green beans, which I plant at will in vacant areas. But you also can plant spinach, beets, turnips, carrots and lettuce.

Green beans are easy because they don't mind the heat. For the others, which grow best in cooler weather, you'll need to be careful. Tiny sprouts of spinach and lettuce need to be kept wet and, if possible, cool. The hot wind and 100-degree joy of August in Kansas City won't do.

I've never been very successful at getting second crops from these vegetables. But people who have tell me they try to put the little greens in the shade of something bigger (but not too aggressive) and keep them watered.

Chapter 9:
Pests: Four-legged & feathered

That garden of yours looks great. Then one day you peer out the window and notice something odd, troubling and…oh, my God!

That stand of sweet corn you're so proud of? It's convulsing, as if the stalks are having a violent fit because some…thing…is…in…there!

Or maybe some suppertime you venture out to grab tender fresh greens for a salad, only to discover that something got there first.

Or, hungry for a BLT, you approach the tomato plants, drooling at the sight of those juicy red monsters on the vine. But then you notice that the ripest fruit is starting to rot because some no-good, bushy-tailed vandal has taken one bite only of the prettiest tomatoes, as if to say, "Heh, heh, take that, loser!"

Gardeners are always at war with varmints: rabbits, squirrels, raccoons, deer and more. But here's the good news:

Over the years, Roxie and I have put our giant brains together and triumphed over some pests, achieved an uneasy truce with others and learned to cope as best we can with one bushy-tailed counterinsurgency that shows no signs of giving up.

Oh, those bleeping squirrels.

RABBITS

For years, Roxie and I had no problems with rabbits. Whatever damage they caused was minimal.

Then one season, the rabbits picked clean our rows of leafy vegetables. Young lettuce, broccoli and cauliflower plants were stripped before they gained a foothold. We ended up with enough broccoli for a couple of stir-fries.

Why the sudden attention? Could have been a bumper year for the rabbit population. Nature goes through cycles.

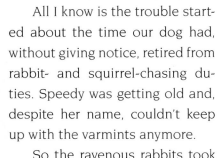

All I know is the trouble started about the time our dog had, without giving notice, retired from rabbit- and squirrel-chasing duties. Speedy was getting old and, despite her name, couldn't keep up with the varmints anymore.

So the ravenous rabbits took advantage of the situation. We tried sprinkling the plants with nasty powders like rotenone, but it didn't work. Nor did liquid repellants or the method some swear by: allowing the radio to blare in the garden overnight.

Our Lenexa rabbits seemed to prefer music and news on the hour while they chewed their greens.

Finally I decided that if we were to keep out rabbits, we'd need a proper fence. We've had no trouble with rabbits since then.

Your fence doesn't have to be as elaborate or time-consuming to build as mine. (*See instructions on Page* 80.) But it must meet two basic requirements:

• It needs to be at least 2 feet tall. Cottontail rabbits can jump, but not that high.

• It needs to be secured to the ground and between sections because little bunnies can squeeze through and under loose fencing (though contrary to what you might have learned from watching Bugs Bunny cartoons, rabbits are not much for digging.)

What kind of fencing? Surround your veggies with 1-inch mesh poultry wire, which you can find at big-box building supply or farm and ranch stores. Some hardware and garden stores carry it, too.

When setting up the galvanized poultry wire, anchor it to the ground with stakes or, better yet, bury an inch or two of it, then allow the grass to grow through for an even more secure enclosure.

Leave space between the fencing and your plants. Otherwise rabbits will nibble through those 1-inch openings in the mesh.

For a small garden, some might choose to fence off individual plants. For our large garden, I went to the trouble of stapling the poultry wire to wooden frames, resulting in a fence that is more stable and attractive than staked-up wire mesh.

I put up my fence in the spring and take it down in fall, carefully numbering each section with a permanent marker. That way I can remember which section goes where the following spring.

We couldn't garden without our rabbit fence. We can tell it's effective by how sad the bunny rabbits look as they peer through the chicken wire at all those greens they're missing out on.

RACCOONS AND GROUNDHOGS

We've never suspected a raccoon of visiting our garden.

Those who do contend with them say one way to scare them off is to leave a radio on at night in the garden. Like Roxie, they are repelled by talk radio, or so it's said.

Think maybe they're liberals? Or is it just that human voices connote danger?

There is a fencing option, but in the case of raccoons, you don't want a strong, rigid fence as you do for deer or rabbits. Gardeners with raccoon problems want a fence that is 6 or 7 feet tall and made out of floppy plastic mesh that is harder for raccoons to climb.

Fencing is also recommended for controlling groundhogs, also known as woodchucks. But here we're talking a far more elaborate fence than the others we've touched on.

When I spotted a groundhog in my yard recently, I figured the rabbit fence would protect the garden. But then I did some research and became worried. The brutes are bigger, stronger and more determined than rabbits. Plus, groundhogs are champion burrowers.

Therefore, if you're worried about groundhogs, you'll need a fence that's about 4 feet tall and has a skirt buried a couple of feet deep. You also might want to electrify it with a nonlethal charge.

Build Mike's rabbit fence

You can keep rabbits out of the garden by staking up poultry wire along the perimeter. But for a finished look, you'll want to build a real fence. These section lengths can be adjusted to fit your space.

INSTRUCTIONS

1. Each rectangular fence section measures 8 feet by 2 feet. For each section: Cut three 22-inch pieces from the 1x2 furring strips. There is a vertical piece for each end of the panel and one for a center support.
2. Secure with finishing nails to two 8-foot pieces of 1x2 furring strips.
3. Repeat for as many frames as necessary to enclose garden. You can adjust the length of one or two sections for a perfect fit, but leave room for the fence posts.
4. Use treated 1x2s, if you can find them. Another option is to buy builder's grade pine and stain it to help preserve the wood. The disadvantage is that the bottom rails eventually rot, but they're easily replaced.
5. Cut poultry mesh to fit frames. Once the stain is dry, staple poultry mesh taut to the frames. Leave about an inch of the fencing hanging over the bottom rail so it will make contact with ground and provide more protection.
6. To install: Drive a 2x2 fence post in one corner. Abut one end of a fence section to the post and secure with wire at the top and bottom. Pound another post at the other end, to which you'll wire the first and second sections, and so on.

MATERIALS

8-foot lengths of 1x2 furring strips, builder's grade. You'll need three 8-foot lengths for each 8-foot section

2-foot-tall galvanized poultry netting with openings no larger than 1 inch. Again, length depends on coverage area.

2 x 2 pressure-treated deck lumber, cut into 32-inch lengths for fence posts. Number depends on number of sections. Cut one end on the diagonal for easy staking.

Heavy-duty staples

2-inch finishing nails

Deck or wood stain

Wire (whatever you have handy)

TOOLS YOU'LL NEED

Claw hammer

Staple gun

Paint brush or sprayer

Live traps are made for varmints of all sizes.

That seemed like more trouble than I was interested in undertaking to deal with one measly groundhog. So I checked with K-State Research and Extension to see what other methods were recommended and came across the following: "A young, medium-size groundhog makes excellent table fare if properly prepared."

No, I couldn't bring myself to shoot him. It's illegal in the city, and, worse, the brochure provided no recipes for groundhog stew. So I did the next best thing and baited a live trap with lettuce.

We have three traps acquired over the years: small, medium and large. I once used the big one, advertised as raccoon size, to catch our cat. (Long story.)

I figured the raccoon/cat trap would work for my groundhog, which was about the size of a large tomcat. My plan was to catch the critter and then transport it to a secret undisclosed location. And it would have worked, I think, except he never showed up for dinner.

One day, groundhog sightings everywhere. In my yard, in the neighbors' yards.

Then, nothing. He seemed to have vanished.

A week later I paid a call on our neighbor Michelle, in whose barn the groundhog had been living, and she, too, was curious what had become of our friend.

"Funny thing is," Michelle said. "The last day I saw him is also the day I saw that fox that comes around every so often."

For a brief happy moment, I figured the Great Circle of Life had come to the rescue of our garden. But no luck. A couple of weeks later the groundhog was back and I was setting out my trap once again.

SQUIRRELS

Squirrels are cute, as readers of my *Kansas City Star* column have told me over the years. They're funny, too — until one chews through the wiring in your attic, starting a fire that leaves you homeless — if you're lucky enough to survive the inferno.

But to our point, they are ravenous pests whose hunger for garden produce has prompted many a tortured urban gardener to give up trying to grow two of the most popular summertime crops, tomatoes and sweet corn.

Let's establish one thing: It is impossible to entirely eradicate the threat to your garden posed by squirrels. Short of setting out poison, which is always dangerous and sometimes illegal, it is beyond human control.

As always, fencing is one option. According to our friends at K-State Research and Extension, such a fence should:

• Be at least 30 inches high and buried 6 inches underground, "with an additional 6 inches bent outward at a 90-degree angle to discourage burrowing."

• Have two electrical wires set off about 3 inches from the fence, one at fence height and the other 2 to 6 inches off the ground.

In other words, the squirrel equivalent of "Stalag 17." All that's missing are the guard towers and William Holden trading cigarettes for favors from the Nazis.

I suppose the squirrels could have one of their pals sacrifice himself for the cause by jumping into a transformer and taking down the power grid temporarily. Still, I might give the electric fence a shot one of these years, though I doubt many average gardeners would be willing to go to the trouble of turning their vegetable patches into a secure area.

What most do instead is deal with the problem as best they can. Some spend a lot of money on supposed squirrel repellants. Pepper spray is popular, as are formulations whose active ingredient is urine, perhaps coyote.

Roxie and I have tried both, and neither worked worth a darn. In fact, our squirrels seem to prefer their tomatoes served spicy with a dash of urine. Plus, you have to reapply the stuff after each rain, which gets to be an expensive hassle.

We've tried the radio trick, but it only wore out the batteries. The squirrels didn't seem to care that Rush Limbaugh was trying to spoil their meal.

Other suggested methods to discourage squirrels that are equally worthless:

• Setting out mothballs.

• Spreading about fur combed from pets.

• Bribing squirrels with decoy food and water, which instead will be viewed as just one more course in the garden feast.

When I wrote a column in early 2009 about the threat that squirrels posed to the White House victory garden, reader Steve Roberson wrote in suggesting trickery as yet another method:

"A friend gave me a tip prior to last year's growing season that I thought I would pass along. Hang red Christmas ornaments on the tomato cages when you set out the plants. By the time tomatoes begin to ripen, the squirrels are already convinced that those round red things are not edible."

Roxie and I are giving that a try.

Meanwhile, we figure it never hurts to have a big dog in the yard to keep the squirrels off kilter. Speedy's replacement is a mutt named Einstein.

It has also become my practice to counter the squirrel threat by taking them for a ride.

When the squirrels become overly interested in the garden, I set out a live trap baited with peanut butter and wait for it to snap shut. Then Mr. Bushy Tail and I drive to the park, where I let him go.

Some people say this method, too, is useless, because eventually another squirrel will take over the territory of the one that was removed. Maybe so. But I think it got rid of the more aggressive garden moochers.

Another argument against the practice: cruelty. Squirrels supposedly have a hard time making a go of it in a new territory already claimed by other squirrels.

But there are worse fates.

My friend "Fred" was an avid gardener until until he reached his 90s. He lived three houses down from us and dealt with the same posse of squirrels we did. Yet Fred claimed to have the problem licked, so one day I asked for his secret.

"I give them swimming lessons," he said, cracking a grin. "In a rain barrel. Turns out, they can't swim."

Their last resting place? The very garden they'd visited without an invitation. "They make good fertilizer," Fred said.

I told that story in a 1998 newspaper column. I may still be getting angry calls from squirrel lovers.

DEER

Our place is too far within the city — and too surrounded with concrete — for us to have had trouble with Bambi.

Fake out squirrels by hanging Christmas ornaments amid the tomatoes.

But those who do live in deer country tell us the best and only way to keep deer from invading a vegetable garden is with a proper fence.

"Otherwise, you might as well not even try to grow anything," says our friend Victor. He lives in Lenexa near Shawnee Mission Park, which is overrun with deer.

Urban/suburban deer have few predators other than automobiles. So anyone with hopes of growing tomatoes, corn or much of anything in a neighborhood like Victor's has to fence the vegetables in and the deer out.

We're talking a fence that is 7 feet tall, because white-tails can jump that high. They are also strong, so make sure the fence posts are sturdy, and it wouldn't hurt to run nonlethal electrical current in the wire.

Bamboo house designed as corn-crop savior BY ROXIE

Sometimes a garden isn't just a garden. Sometimes it is performance art.

Imagine yourself on display in a large, open cage. The day is hot. A gentle breeze blows.

You are holding the bamboo rod of what looks like a large TinkerToy structure high above your head. As you push one end into a connector, the other end of the rod falls out. You hurry over and fix that one, but that skews the connection at another point and you have to run, like a circus plate spinner, to catch it before it falls. Sweat drips into your eyes. Corn leaves slap you in the face. Nylon netting catches on your shirt. You flail and curse.

That is the type of show our neighbors might have taken in, had they looked out a window and seen Mike in midsummer a couple years ago.

Had we sold tickets, we might have titled it "Varmints' Revenge."

Season after season, just as the corn was almost ready, the story was the same. We'd go out and find the beautiful ears we'd been watching stripped clean. Sometimes we'd see the tassels shaking and catch one of those tree rats in the act. But the scare was never enough to keep them away for long.

The corn "building" sounds like one of my crazy schemes, but in fact it was entirely Mike's idea. The concept: A loose structure of bamboo and bird netting, weighted at the ground, would keep the squirrels out of the corn. What could be simpler?

He looked through some catalogs, ordered the supplies and went to work. When it was up it looked...well, it looked a bit rickety.

But here's the important part: It worked. As long as there was no wind whatsoever.

This being Kansas City, you know about how long that lasted. Mike swore at the corn house nearly every day. Some days he had the gruesome chore of extracting dead ground squirrels or birds from the netting. Other times the mud caused the poles to twist and the netting to drop.

Finally, a big gust in the middle of the night sealed the deal. The netting and the corn were both on the ground the next day.

We don't grow sweet corn anymore.

BIRDS

Remember that Alfred Hitchcock flick "The Birds"? I first saw it when I was 9 or 10, and all that screaming horror convinced me that birds could do some real damage. They could even peck your eyes out!

But what cinched it for me was one spring, decades later, when the birds descended on our garden. Not sure what Roxie and I did to offend them. But with cruel and malicious precision, birds horribly mutilated two perfectly fine stands of sweet corn.

Years later the birds came after us again, during spring when we least expected it, and savaged our young plants, snipping off the tender stems at ground level.

Hanging CDs from the branches helps scare away birds from fruit trees.

So we know a thing or two about the damage birds can do. We have a few tips:

• In early spring, set out a bunch of twigs or a bale of straw. It's better than having birds visit your garden in search of nesting material. As soon as the plants are big and hardy, usually by late May, feel free to tidy up.

• The black plastic mesh sold as bird netting in stores is effective in keeping birds away from apples, cherries, berries and corn. However, netting isn't cheap and is frustrating to use. If possible, have a helper to prevent snagging.

• Hang bright, shiny, noisy things. We dangle pie tins, bread tins, old compact discs and even a disco ball in the branches of our fruit trees in hopes of scaring away the birds from our apples and cherries.

• Another bright, shiny and not so noisy thing we have used is a "scare eye." It's basically a heavy-duty balloon that comes in bright colors, with reflective "eyes" and streamers that move about in the breeze and supposedly scare birds. Find them advertised online and at some garden stores.

  • We have a plastic owl filled with sand on the fencepost, which looks cool in a kitschy way. Whether it keeps the birds at bay, we'll never know.

  • Humans have been posting scarecrows in their gardens and farm fields since at least 1939, when "The Wizard of Oz" was released. If they only had brains!

Do they keep birds away from crops? We think so, especially if the scarecrow has some unpredictability — armlike streamers that blow in the wind, that sort of thing. Sudden movements spook birds. And if they don't work, well, at least they're sort of fun.

Opposite: Mike found the scarecrow's head during a hunting trip in central Kansas. We added tennis balls for eyes, one of Mike's high-school jackets and a Kansas City Royals cap.

Chapter 10:
More pests:
Bugs, fungi & wilts

As I write this, I'm feeling uneasy about the cucumbers. It's nothing concrete. Just a little twinge I felt yesterday when I noticed one plant seemed to be hanging to its trellis without much verve. It seems a bit early to be fighting off that wilt. But yet …

Let's face it. Nothing about gardening is certain except this: At some point, something will go wrong with the plants.

Playing plant doctor is a skill that takes a few seasons to develop. Even after 25 seasons of periodically droopy cukes, I'll probably still rush to my source books or the Internet or other gardeners to find hope of staving off whatever it is.

We don't have space in this book to give the lowdown on every bug, leaf blight or bacterial wilt, their causes and treatments. (*There are some very good sources out there. See our recommendations on Page* 128.) But here is our best overall advice: Look at your plants every day.

I can't emphasize enough how important it is to look closely at the plants, even when you don't think there is a problem. It is much easier to determine that slugs are at your lettuce if you actually turn over a leaf and catch one in the act.

Just like medical diagnoses, the earlier you catch a problem, the better chance your garden has of recovery. The longer you wait, the more costly, time-consuming and toxic the solution will be.

When something doesn't look right, it usually comes down to one of three things: water, disease or bugs. I used to think those three things were equally likely. Experience, however, has taught me that a water problem speeds along the bugs, and a disease problem often was caused by bugs. So now I just assume it's a bug problem to save time.

One of our very early gardening years was during a horrific drought. Every day I noticed that the leaves on the green beans seemed browner. I assumed this was drought-related, so I watered them. They were in bloom, so I figured that would take care of it.

They kept getting browner, and I kept watering. By the time I noticed the webbing, it was too late. I read later that spider mites were my culprits. Spider mites are very happy with dry conditions and, as their name implies, they are all but invisible to the naked eye. They destroyed both rows of beans that year.

So, two lessons: Rolled leaves are a better sign of a thirsty plant than brown leaves. And you don't actually have to see the bugs. Just assume they are there.

Here is a short list of the top problems we've encountered over the years. This is by no means exhaustive. Your garden may be in a very different microculture.

Plant suddenly looks wilted; no bugs evident. I've gotten this year after year in the cucumber bed. This is actually a disease — a bacterial wilt transmitted by the spotted or striped cucumber beetle as it bites the leaves. Unfortunately, I never notice the bugs until too late, because the spotted beetle looks a lot like a ladybug.

Once a plant starts to wilt you can't save it, but you may be able to save its neighbors by controlling the bugs. The best weapon I've tried is a powder containing pyrethrins.

As for the afflicted plant, don't bother pulling it out. The bacteria need an open wound to spread, so the plants can't catch it from one another. This wilt also can affect other vining plants, including squash, melons and pumpkins.

Bedding plants you set out with such pride are cut off at the base of the stem. The first time this happened, I was sure it was the work of some psychopathic broccoli hater or malicious kid. But neighbors told me it was cutworms, probably carried into the garden in the load of manure we spread the previous fall. Cutworms waste an entire plant for the little they eat at the stem.

Brown or yellow mottled leaves dry out and die. First suspect: spider mites. Don't wait to see the webbing. The mites sometimes look like dust on the leaf back. One way to see them (if they're the red kind) is to shake leaves over a piece of paper.

Broccoli, cauliflower and cabbage heads have green slime in the florets. Don't call the Ghostbusters. These are the eggs of the cabbage worm looper, a white or yellow winged moth you may have admired a few days ago. They hatch into green worms whose bodies will turn up in the water in which you blanch the vegetables. If you don't want your kids to see this and forever refuse to eat broccoli, you need to get rid of them.

Tomato leaves turn brown and wilt from the bottom up. This could be a fungus caused by poor air circulation. After one particularly bad year, I decided to plant my tomatoes in long rows rather than a grid. We haven't had a problem since.

A tomato that suddenly wilts and dies also could be reacting to a chemical washed off the leaves of a nearby

Tomatoes may fall victim to viral or bacterial wilts.

black walnut tree. Or it could be victim of any number of viral or bacterial wilts. Most hybrids have some bred-in resistance, but older types may not.

Fusarium wilt, verticillium wilt, tobacco mosaic: There are ways to tell which kind of wilt you have, but to me, it's all academic. The only thing you can do at this point is pull the wilted plant as soon as possible. Some experts say the heat in the middle of the compost pile will kill the viruses or bacteria. But we don't take chances on spreading the disease the following year, so we don't compost the plants. Make sure to move your tomato patch to a different part of the garden next year.

PLAN OF ACTION

As I said, every garden gets bugs. Whether those bugs will become a problem depends a little bit on where you live.

If you are near a wooded area, you have a better chance of beating the bugs. Where there are trees, there are birds, and possibly beneficial bugs and bats. These natural predators eat the bad bugs, which makes your life a whole lot easier. So don't be too hard on that neighbor with a broken shed window. It could be a home for bats.

My first choice, after seeing a potential problem, is to do nothing. This is not only from laziness. It just seems that some problems will take care of themselves if left alone.

I keep a careful eye on the situation, and if it quickly gets worse, I have a protocol that goes from least to most toxic:

Pick the bugs or their eggs by hand and squish them. Hand-to-hand combat is one of the least lethal and most entertaining ways to deal with a pest problem. For instance, if you suspect slugs, leave out a plate or brick nearby. Slugs will congregate underneath, so you can take them on a little voyage to the garbage can.

Barriers and traps. Just like college students, slugs are attracted to beer. Sink a container or saucer into the dirt so just a bit projects above ground level. Then fill it with beer. Slugs will happily flock to the beer — and to their deaths. At least they died partying, is how I see it.

One gardening book I consulted said slugs also could be repelled by laying copper sheeting on the ground around the trouble spot. The theory is that the copper reacts with their slime and gives them a little electric shock. Cool as this sounds, I couldn't see myself doing it. Given the price of scrap copper, it wouldn't be there long.

Cutworms are another bug that is deterred by a barrier. A friend says she deals with them by sticking a nail close to the stem of each bedding plant. That way, she said, the worm can't wrap completely around to cut the plant. Other sources recommend collars made from paper, or tuna cans with bottom and top removed.

I didn't want to pick all that sharp metal out of the garden, so instead I put two small twigs next to the stem instead of nails. Never had a problem since.

Other bugs can be fended off with row covers supported by wire. These essentially keep moths from getting to the plants to lay eggs. I've never used them, though, because of the expense, the trouble of looking under them to inspect the plants and the likelihood the Kansas wind will blow them into the next county.

Insecticidal soap. Once you begin going to the store shelves for a solution, it's best to start reading labels. I look for indoor/outdoor products that can be used on vegetables right up to the day of harvest. The active ingredients in insecticidal soap

are potassium salts and fatty acids, and the soap is effective against many of the most common bugs in the Kansas City area.

Praying mantises and ladybugs will attack the bugs you want to get rid of.

Bacillus thuringiensis (Bt). This is another spray that is especially effective against moths and caterpillars. It has next to no impact on humans, wildlife or beneficial insects and is considered environmentally friendly. We've used it on broccoli, cauliflower, corn and our apple trees. It goes under the names Dipel or Thuricide. Sci-

entists have genetically engineered some crops to contain Bt, and experts now worry that these crops will create pressure for insects to become resistant. So enjoy it while you can.

Pyrethrin dust and Rotenone. These are products of last resort because they are more toxic to fish and wildlife than the previous products. Read the label carefully before applying.

One more solution to the bug problem has become increasingly popular the last few years — bug predators. Once considered an oddity, they are now quite common at garden stores. Ladybugs, praying mantises and beneficial nematodes all will attack the bugs you want to get rid of.

I've never tried this, but it looks like fun. If only you could train them to stay put.

Chapter 11:
Seed saving

Every year about mid-July, we get the same question from our kids as they pass the kitchen sink: "What's that awful smell?"

To which I utter the same reply my grandparents used to give when we passed a feedlot: "Smells like money."

Actually, the stinky process we use to save our own tomato seeds doesn't save us tons of money. We do it because it's fun and because we can. A dollar is a dollar, after all.

The first thing to know about seed saving is that it won't work for everything you plant. If you planted hybrids for disease resistance, the seeds you save will not be the hybrid you wanted. They will be one of its ancestors.

You can save standard varieties, such as heirlooms. If you do, watch out for cross-pollination. If you have more than one variety of, say, sweet corn and they are planted fairly close together, they could pollinate each other and, again, the seeds you get won't give you exactly the roasting ear you want.

I plant a fair number of hybrids and sometimes have more than one type of each vegetable in the garden too close together. Even so, I save the Roma paste tomatoes and sometimes an heirloom Brandywine most years. The proximity of the different types to one another means the seed stock becomes a little more corrupted each year. So every four or five years, I start fresh with a new packet.

HOW TO SAVE SEEDS

Cut open ripe tomatoes and scoop out the seeds and gel into juice glasses. Let the glasses sit at room temperature a few days until they get a little mold on top and a funky smell. At that point, carefully pour off the scum and floating seeds and add a little water.

The next day, pour off as much water as you can without disturbing the seeds on the bottom. Add a little more water and let stand. Repeat daily until you have nearly clear water and seeds with no tomato residue.

Pour what's left on a clean plate. Spread the seeds and let dry completely. Scrape the seeds into a plastic storage bag and label for next season.

Of course, that isn't the only way. Some people scoop the seeds and gel onto a paper towel and let the whole thing dry, then tear out the seeds to plant next season.

Other seeds can be saved successfully with not as much work. We've saved Moon and Stars watermelon, dill and cilantro seeds by collecting them and letting them dry. For a resource on proven seed-saving methods, try *Seed to Seed: Seed Saving and Growing Techniques for Vegetable Gardeners* (Seed Savers Exchange, 2002) by Suzanne Ashworth.

For some, saving seeds is not just about money. It's a higher calling. Seed Savers Exchange is an excellent group that has been around 35 years and is the largest nongovernmental seed bank in the United States. It was started out of a concern that large-scale agriculture's emphasis on mass-production eventually would cause older varieties of crops to become extinct.

Seed Savers Exchange is one of the top reasons that garden catalogs now have special sections devoted to heirloom vegetables. A $35 membership gives access to thousands of heirloom vegetables, fruits and herbs that are not in the commercial catalogs, as well as a discount on purchases (www. seedsavers.org).

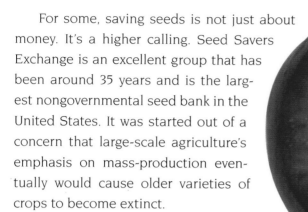

Chapter 12:
Tools of the trade

If I lived off Daddy's trust fund or had no intention of ever paying off the Visa card (can you get away with that?), I'd buy two of everything in the tool aisle at my garden store.

There's some mighty cool stuff hanging on the wall. Next to the regular shovels and hoes hangs an "ergonomically designed weeding tool" that, with its green handle, sort of resembles a space alien. At $48, it has a pretty far-out price, too.

On a shelf near plain-cotton garden gloves that sell for a couple of dollars is a $33 pair that reaches the elbows and is advertised as "thorn and bramble proof!"

As for all those gadgets in the catalog — *ay caramba*! Forget buying groceries. What I wouldn't give for my very own Garden Weasel, or a mini tiller from Mantis.

Problem is, most of us don't have a fortune to spend on fancy, handcrafted garden tools or neat specialty items that, repeat after me, you simply do not need to grow vegetables. And who has room for all that stuff, anyway?

Over the years, Roxie and I have found that you don't need many tools to plant, tend and harvest a veggie garden. The ones you do need, you can pick up for very little money at most any hardware store, or even by cruising garage sales.

That heavy-duty, $80 spade from Wolverine sure would be nice. But I got a perfectly good one for $1 at a garage sale in Roeland Park, Kan.

We still use the old-timey push plow that a neighbor gave us 20 years ago. Same with the 50-year-old David Bradley walk-behind garden tractor, complete with harrow, moldboard plow, planter and snow blade, that a co-worker wanted to get rid of.

Wouldn't take a dime for it, either.

But however you lay your hands on them, there are certain must-have tools for working a decent-sized patch.

Let's start with hoes. Don't be silly. You know the kind I mean. You'll need at least one hoe to uproot or scrape away weeds, as well as to loosen the soil for watering or planting. But it's better to have two or three types of hoes for different types of jobs.

For planting, our weapon of choice is the classic, lightweight **garden hoe** with the iconic rectangular-shape head. Roxie uses ours to dig furrows and then cover the seeds. She wouldn't do without one.

I rarely use that hoe, because a) the only crop I plant is garlic, and then I use a garden trowel for digging the holes, and b) I prefer other hoes when it comes to keeping the garden rows free of weeds.

Top of the list for that is a **stirrup hoe**. Other names for it include action hoe, loop hoe or scuffle hoe. Whatever the store or catalog calls it, you know you have the right tool in your arsenal if the business end resembles the stirrup on a saddle.

The beauty of the design is that it's easy on your back and shoulders and gets the job done quickly when the soil is dry or just moist. Whether you pull it toward you or push it away (the blade is sharp on both sides), the stirrup hoe cuts weeds at the root but leaves all the vegetation and heavy dirt behind.

The classic hoe that Roxie favors also works for light weeding, just not as well.

A stirrup hoe isn't handy for every job. For later in the season, when weeds get more aggressive and the stalks tougher because you got lazy and let the garden get out of hand, it's good to have a **grape hoe**.

The blade alone weighs 2 pounds. And at 8 inches wide, it can do plenty of damage to the weeds and anything else with which it comes in contact.

This page (from left): Warren hoe, grape hoe. Opposite page (from left): garden hoe, stirrup hoe.

You know those murder mysteries where it turns out the gardener did it? It's a good guess he did it with a grape hoe — and one clean blow to the head.

The triangle or **Warren hoe** is good for close-in cultivation. Since the blade comes to a point, it allows for greater precision. Before we got one, I was always clipping off young tomato plants accidentally with a stirrup or grape hoe. Now I slaughter innocent plants only some of the time.

Finally, a **three-prong cultivator** comes in handy for scratching up hard soil.

Other tools you may need include a **garden fork** for harvesting potatoes or, in small gardens, for turning the soil before planting in spring and when putting the garden to bed for the winter.

We use a fork only for harvesting. Our garden is too big and I'm far too lazy — there's that word again — to dig up every inch by hand. For that I use a **roto-tiller** we bought from Sears more than 20 years ago. It blows oil but still works great because we tune it up every 10 years or so, whether or not it needs it.

Of course, it's a whole lot cheaper to rent a tiller (rates were about $50 a day for a front-tine tiller in 2009) or borrow one from a friend (free, but you really ought to spring for a bottle of wine).

Still, if you plan on becoming a serious gardener, a roto-tiller is well worth the investment. One like ours costs about $400. When you consider that you'll probably use it more than once in a season, it would pay for itself in four years.

Also in our barn you'll find various shovels and other implements of destruction, but the only one remotely essential to gardening is the heavy-toothed **garden rake** for collecting all those weeds we've pulled or cut off with a hoe. And to pick up the pile, I use a six-pronged **pitchfork** and scoop the weeds into a wheelbarrow, though a kid's wagon would work, too. The pitchfork also comes in handy for turning the compost pile.

Chapter 13:
Food processing

Even though things go wrong in the garden every year, we still end up with surpluses, almost in spite of ourselves.

We have all the equipment necessary to can, freeze and dry. But, with the exception of pickles and tomatoes, we preserve most vegetables by freezing. Here's why:

I tend to be a worrier. An obsessive, unrelenting worrier — especially when it comes to the idea of feeding my family deadly botulism, which cannot be smelled or seen. So if I decide to use the pressure canner, I'll get out the latest, most updated canning guides from the USDA and follow them to the letter.

Months later, I'll get out that jar of green beans and look it over, testing and retesting the seal. I'll be filled with doubt: Did I remember every step? Was my work surface pristine? How can I be so sure the pressure gauge was working? I'll feel compelled to boil the beans hard for 20 minutes, which is supposed to kill any suspicious toxins. Then we'll eat. But did I really boil them hard enough? Did I time it right?

For the next 36 hours, I'll watch my family closely. Does anyone have a strange headache? Blurred vision or upset stomach? Problems with balance?

I usually decide pressure canning is not worth it, if only because I don't think I could handle the cable news stories that would follow the tragic deaths of everyone in my house. If I survived.

That said, pressure canning of low-acid vegetables is not terribly hard if you slavishly follow the directions. I've pressure-canned green beans, sweet potatoes and beets with no problem. (For more complete instructions on canning, check out the

When the hard times come, there's nothing so soothing as a larder fully stocked.

USDA's *Complete Guide to Home Canning* or the *Ball Blue Book Guide to Preserving*.)

Most vegetables taste better frozen anyway. The canning process cooks the life out of them and heats up the house in the process. Although you have to cook most vegetables at least a few minutes before freezing them, the cooking time is nothing compared with the process of sealing them into glass jars.

THE FREEZING PROCESS

To prepare most vegetables for the freezer, wash them, slice off any bad parts or stems and cut them into uniform pieces. You'll need a large pot, preferably with a basket insert and lid; a colander; and a clean sink full of cold water. A salad spinner helps get rid of the last bit of moisture but is optional.

From there the process is simple. Bring water in the pot to boiling, add a batch of vegetables and boil the required time. When done, carefully lift out the basket insert and dump the vegetables into the colander, which is sitting in the cold water. Swirl around or add more cold water for an equal number of minutes, or until the vegetables are no longer hot. This is called "blanching."

Run the vegetables through the salad spinner, if you have one, and lay them on a clean towel to dry for a bit. Pack them into freezer bags, working out as much air as possible before sealing. Label with an indelible marker and put them along the side walls of the freezer, where they'll freeze fastest.

Boiling time varies by density and size. Here are a few of the most common vegetables listed by University of Missouri Extension. Don't forget to plunge the cooked vegetables immediately into cold water.

Green or wax beans: 3 minutes

Lima, butter or pinto beans: 2 minutes for small, 3 minutes for medium and 4 minutes for large

Broccoli: Cut into 1½-inch florets. To get rid of bugs, soak 30 minutes in a brine of 4 teaspoons salt to 1 gallon water. Boil 3 minutes.

Brussels sprouts: Small heads, 3 minutes; medium heads, 4 minutes; and large heads, 5 minutes.

Cauliflower: Cut into 1-inch pieces and brine as for broccoli. Boil 3 minutes in 4 teaspoons salt per 1 gallon water. Adding 2 or 3 tablespoons lemon juice to the cooking water will keep the cauliflower white.

Corn: I like the cream-style corn you get by cutting the kernels off the cob and then scraping the cobs with the back of the knife. Cook the corn in the top of a double boiler with no added liquid about 10 minutes and cool by putting the pan in ice water.

Corn on the cob can be frozen, but I've never had any I loved from the freezer. To do that, you have to have a pot big enough to fit the entire ear. Boil small ears 7 minutes; medium ears 9 minutes; and large ones 11 minutes.

Sweet peas: Boil 1½ minutes.

Some vegetables can be frozen without much prep at all, and every year I give thanks for them. Peppers can be frozen cut or whole after only washing and cutting out any bad spots. Onions and shallots must be skinned first, which is a pain, then chopped and stored in freezer bags. Chopped shallots also freeze well in ice cube trays, resulting in recipe-size portions.

I don't freeze beets, carrots or other root vegetables, because they keep well in a cool place, such as a root cellar or refrigerator. Simply wash and dry them first.

White and sweet potatoes need exposure to air to cure after harvesting, but they, too, will last a long time in a cool place without processing. Same with butternut squash. Do not store squash or potatoes in the fridge if you want to keep them any length of time.

THE WATER BATH METHOD

For foods with high acidity (tomatoes and pickles) or sugar content (jellies and jams), use a water bath canner. High acid and sugar are the natural enemies of botulism, so I feel safe doing this.

You don't need a pressure canner for the water bath method. But you will need some equipment: A lidded pot large enough to hold your jars, covered by at least an inch of water; a rack for the pot bottom (I have a round cake rack in mine); a jar lifter (special tongs that grab the neck of a canning jar); regular tongs; and canning jars with new bands and lids.

Most of these items can be found at a hardware store. Grocery stores usually carry at least the bands and lids. Bands can be reused, but you'll need brand-new lids every time for a proper seal.

I bought lots of jars starting out, but I was a fool. I learned that many people have surplus canning jars in their garages and basements and are happy to unload them for free. After a while, I quit accepting handouts. Make sure you get real canning jars, which are made of glass that can withstand heat without cracking.

I usually can the tomatoes as a thin puree because it can be used in marinara sauce, tomato soup or enchilada sauce. Complete instructions for the water bath method and others can be found in the USDA *Complete Guide to Home Canning* (2006 revision) or the *Ball Blue Book of Preserving*. But here is the general procedure:

Sterilize the jars, bands and lids in boiling water, then fill the jars with puree, jelly or pickles. Screw on the lids and boil the jars the amount of time specified in the recipe.

THE PICKLING PROCESS

My favorite time is pickle-making season. I can some pickles in the water bath. But I also have a couple of easy favorites that simply go into a brine and into the refrigerator.

Pail Pickles

Makes 2 quarts

12 medium pickling cucumbers, scrubbed and sliced thin (see note)

1 large onion, sliced thin

½ green pepper, sliced thin

2 cups white vinegar

⅓ cup salt, noniodized

1 teaspoon celery seed

3 cups sugar

Combine cucumber, onion and green pepper slices. Heat remaining ingredients over medium heat until sugar and salt are dissolved; pour over the vegetables. After mixture has cooled, transfer to 2 wide-mouth quart jars. Should keep several weeks in the refrigerator.

Note: Avoid cucumbers that have grown large and have yellowed. They will be floppy and seedy.

Recipes This pickle recipe is a family favorite of Mike's Wisconsin relatives. It was sent to me by his sister, Jodi Coppens of Green Bay. It is a very flexible recipe that calls for a small ice cream pail, but since I never have room in the refrigerator, I use quart jars. It also calls for green peppers, but sometimes I leave them out. (Sorry, Jodi.) I've modified the recipe to include more precise amounts. —*Roxie*

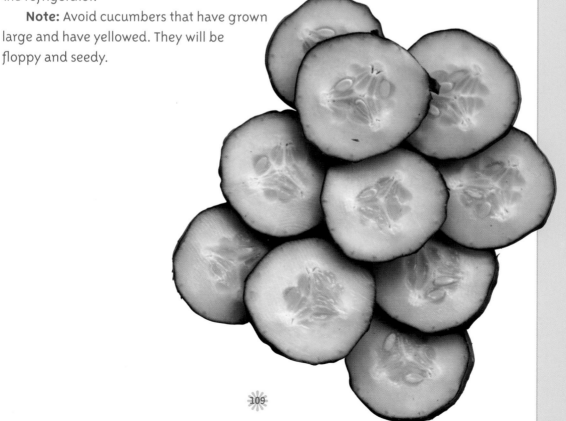

Zippy Dill Slices

I adapted my dill pickle recipe from one I clipped out of a magazine years ago.

Makes 2 quarts
12 large pickling cucumbers
1 small onion, thinly sliced
1 small carrot, thinly sliced
1 or 1½ large jalapeno peppers (enough so there's ½ in each jar), cut in half lengthwise
Fresh dill bunches (the flowering heads), enough to put some in each jar
4 cups water
3 cups white vinegar
6 tablespoons kosher salt
2 tablespoons sugar
1½ teaspoons black pepper
¾ teaspoon ground ginger
¾ teaspoon ground cumin
¾ teaspoon turmeric
3 whole cloves
1 large bay leaf

Wash cucumbers and scrub off the prickly spines. Cut off and discard the ends, then slice thinly into a large, nonreactive bowl. Add onion, carrot, jalapeno and dill.

Bring water, vinegar, salt, sugar and spices to a boil. Pour mixture over the cucumbers, onion and carrot. Let stand at room temperature 24 hours before putting into 2 sterile wide-mouthed quart jars. Store in refrigerator at least a week before serving. Should keep several weeks in the refrigerator.

Pesto Genovese

Makes about 1 cup

2 cups fresh basil leaves

½ cup olive oil

2 tablespoons pine nuts or other nuts, such as English walnuts

2 cloves garlic, peeled

½ cup grated Parmesan cheese

Salt to taste

Prepare 2 plastic ice cube trays by poking plastic sandwich wrap into each cube. This will make it easier to remove the pesto after it has frozen.

Rinse basil in 3 successive bowls of water, until all grit is gone. Remove excess water in a salad spinner. Combine basil, olive oil, nuts and garlic in food processor and puree. Remove to another bowl; stir in cheese and salt to taste. Spoon into trays, cover and freeze. This will make about 1½ trays.

When the pesto is frozen, remove the cubes and store in labeled freezer bags. To serve, defrost overnight in the refrigerator.

Chapter 14:
Fall cleanup

Each spring, we can hardly wait to get our hands dirty in the garden. And every fall, we can't wait to tell the garden goodbye until next year.

Oh, how we long for that first hard freeze so we can take a break from our garden chores.

That explains why, if you were to visit our garden toward mid-September, you would notice a striking sense of ennui had set in. There would be more weeds than a month earlier.

Also, the ground would be littered with overripe tomatoes because we quit picking them, except for the occasional salad or Italian dish.

When Roxie is through processing plum tomatoes for sauce and frozen roasted tomatoes, we have little use for all those Romas, especially the late-season runts, which are punier than the fruit produced at high season.

By mid- to late September, we've also let the broccoli go to seed. I've long since yanked up the last cauliflower plants, chopped them to bits with a machete and tossed the pieces into the compost pile.

Come to think of it, the late garden is something of an eyesore. Some gardeners have successful second-season crops growing by then. But we've never been big on fall gardening. About all that is still flourishing late in the year in our garden are the basil and pepper plants, as well as the sweet potato vines.

When that first freeze is forecast, I'm happy to dig the sweet potatoes, pick the last peppers and chop basil for drying in the basement.

Garlic planted in fall stands out against a dusting of snow.

Whatever mistakes we made or disappointments we experienced during the growing season are soon erased from sight — if not from memory — in the flurry of garden cleanup.

Down comes the rabbit fence, which I'm careful to number with permanent marker so I can remember which section goes where when spring comes. The fence sections I stack in the loft of our barn to protect the wood from the weather. I make note of the repairs the fence needs, promise myself I'll do the work in the winter — and then put it off until spring.

Next, I stow the tomato cages. To save space, I flatten them by stomping on them. Then I pile them up outside. Because they're made of galvanized steel, rust is not a concern.

Next comes the fun part. I uproot all the remaining garden plants and toss them in the composter. Then I mow the weeds and grasses that I've allowed to grow out of control.

It's now late October or early November, time to pick up a shovel and add nutrients to the soil for next year. We fertilize only in fall, although some gardeners fertilize more often.

I spread any compost that's broken down to resemble dirt, as well as any composted manure (never chemical fertilizers) I've scored free from friends who stable horses or from people advertising it for sale. One year I paid $50 for a pickup load. The newspaper classified ads and Craigslist are good places to look.

I don't add manure and compost right away because we have a fine old tradition at our place. After the growing season, we invite the neighbors to a garden party. We cook brats and burgers. Libations are consumed. And the centerpiece is a roaring bonfire that we set ablaze smack in the center of the garden. (I scoop up the ashes later so the ashes don't disrupt the pH balance of the soil.) Since our guests might not appreciate stepping in manure while they toast their marshmallows, we wait until after the party to fertilize.

This means I till the garden twice after the growing season — once before the party for purely aesthetic reasons, and once after to work in nutrients.

At this point, I would be through with my garden chores until March, when Roxie kicks off yet another promising garden season by planting potatoes. But a few years ago we learned what everyone else already knew: The best time to plant garlic is autumn.

And the best way to plant garlic? Pointy-side up and 4 to 6 inches deep, rather than the 1 to 2 inches some recommend. Shallow plantings don't always survive the sometime bitter winter temperatures in Kansas City.

Planting that deep means you end up doing much of the work on your hands and knees. In horse manure. But, hey! Life would not be worth living without fresh garlic.

Or gardening, for that matter.

Chapter 15:
Counting our savings

The garden season is over. The last sweet potatoes have been dug and the canning equipment put away. When we finally have a moment to sit, we ask ourselves this burning question: Did all that work save us any money?

At the end of 2008, after working especially hard all summer, I was feeling a little down. Had I been wasting my time all these years, being the oddball who cans her own salsa and pickles? I always assumed that gardening saved money, but did it really?

To make myself feel better, I decided to keep track of all the food I processed. I tallied the bags of frozen vegetables and the filled canning jars, including jams and jellies. Then I went to the store with a pad and pen and tried to find equivalent products and their costs.

And the answer is...yes, we did save money.

Before I tell you how much, you need to know a couple of things. This figure does not include food that we harvested for immediate use, such as spinach, radishes and lettuce. I wasn't focused enough for that. Vegetables we didn't process at all, including onions, herbs (except basil), beets, carrots and white potatoes, also are not included in the total.

That means the total is low, although it is balanced somewhat by the fact that I also did not keep track of things I had to buy to do the processing — a couple of bags of sugar, a gallon of vinegar, olive oil, canning lids and, oh, that bottle of brandy for the brandied cherries that will become chocolate-covered for Christmas.

So...drum roll, please...we saved $496.52. Of that, $54.96 was from products made from our cherry and two apple trees (which never produce that well), red currant bush and grapevine. The rest, $441.56, was from vegetables and strawberries alone.

Looking through the list, the priciest items are the tomato salsa, dried tomatoes, pickles and pesto. With basil pesto going for 79 cents an ounce, it definitely is worth it to grind and freeze our own. Making just two batches (15 pints) of salsa — with only lemon juice and a little tomato paste not from the garden — saved us close to $50. Home-canned tomato puree saved about $90, and pickles, $77.

So there you have it. Maybe we didn't become millionaires by growing our own food. But we do have some other things. We have satisfying work. We have pure food. We have an interesting menu. We have kids who like broccoli.

We have $496.52. And in hard times, we have happiness and joy.

We have our brave little garden, and it has seen us through.

Opposite: A potato plant stretches for the sun.

Chapter 16:
Saving the Earth

Keeping a garden touches an ancient nerve.

We may spend most of our time in that fast-paced, air-conditioned state of busyness we've been taught to think of as normal. We may tell ourselves we are satisfied. Yet in our time off, when we are most honest with ourselves, who among us doesn't yearn for nature?

For many, a backyard vegetable garden starts as a way to save money and gain dietary control. Then it grows into something else. It becomes an educational tool, a city beautification project, a protection against urban poverty, a stand against global warming. A backyard vegetable garden becomes, in essence, a small step to save humankind from its own excesses, to tear down that fence between us and nature that was erected so long ago.

Allow us to introduce you to four Kansas Citians doing just that. In their way, they are trying to save the Earth one brave little garden at a time.

STEVE MANN GARDENS TO GUARANTEE THE FUTURE

The unhealthful Western diet. The loss of community. The end of plentiful oil. Global warming. Steve Mann of Platte Prairie Farms takes aim at them all with his community garden program.

Until 2008, Mann worked at Sprint. He learned to garden as a child at his grandfather's side. "He was my hero and I always wanted to be a farmer, even if I didn't realize

Opposite: Steve Mann

it sometimes," Mann says. When Sprint offered buyouts, Mann jumped at the chance to do what he'd always wanted, deep down.

Mann runs Platte Prairie Farms, his own 2½-acre spread, plus a CSA (Community Supported Agriculture). His "in your yard" CSA, which includes an area around North Kansas City and Riverside, Mo., allows people to buy memberships for a weekly bag of fresh garden produce. But there's more. You can forgo the membership fee if you agree to have a garden on your land and make a small commitment in hours tending it. Mann then designs a no-till plot and does more maintenance.

After only a couple of years, he has close to 9,000 square feet from seven or eight different gardens.

In return for their garden plots, members get a share of the produce, not just from their land but from the others' as well. A share of the produce also goes to Mann for his work and expertise. It's a winning situation for everyone, Mann says, because along with the lettuce and sweet peas, people gain a sense of community.

The environment also gets a boost. Mann's no-till method saves water and energy. Any unsold produce is donated to Harvesters food bank and the Society of St. Andrews, a charitable organization that salvages excess produce from farmers to feed the hungry.

"The best projection is that in Kansas City we get 4 percent of our food locally," he says. "I'd like to see it become 40 or 50 percent. I'd like to see people turning their TVs off, getting out of their chairs and talking to their neighbors, exercising."

Not only will gardening improve people's health, he says, but it will help us deal with coming shortages of energy when we deplete the oil supply.

"It's going to be a 'Mad Max' world," he says. "I get energy from the future, thinking I have to do something to make this not happen."

ALAN BRANHAGEN'S LESSON: FOOD DOESN'T START OUT SHRINK-WRAPPED

For Alan Branhagen and the rest of the staff at Powell Gardens in Kingsville, Mo., gardening is all about education. Branhagen, a horticulturist who oversees Powell's Heartland Harvest Garden, seeks to reinforce for visitors that food comes from the soil rather than the supermarket.

More than 2,000 species of plants, from tomatoes to a cacao tree, grow in the Heartland Harvest Garden, which opened in 2009. Sections in the 12-acre plot illus-

Alan Branhagen is a horticulturist who oversees Powell Gardens' Heartland Harvest Garden (left).

trate many aspects of food production, from row crops such as milo and soybeans to backyard fruit trees.

One area of raised beds shows off heirlooms with names such as "cream sausage" tomatoes. The garden also features tasting stations and a restaurant with the garden's bounty on the menu.

"We're hoping this will impress people to try new things, learn where food comes from," Branhagen says.

Kids who have never seen how a green bean or radish grows may be leery of them. "Children are more likely to eat healthy if they know where food comes from," he says.

Exhibits on the origins of licorice and popcorn also are aimed at kids. But the Heartland Harvest Garden also teaches about sustainable farming methods, diversity, seed starting and nutrition.

Any food not sold in the restaurant is donated to Harvesters food bank.

BROOKE SALVAGGIO CHAMPIONS URBAN SELF-SUFFICIENCY

"Self-sufficiency" is the watchword at Bad Seed, a tiny farmers market at 1909 McGee Street in Kansas City's Crossroads district. You can buy food there, sure. But the organizer, Brooke Salvaggio, has a bigger vision. She'd like to see people start their own gardens, learn how to make things for themselves and connect with the land.

For Salvaggio, homesteading is where it's at. The market has become not only a vending place for urban growers, but also a hub for those interested in learning old-school self-reliance. You can sign up for classes on canning and preserving, beer brewing, compost toilets and herbal medicine, to name a few. The most popular has been "Intro to Urban Homesteading," which is an overview of self-sufficiency techniques, she says.

"Folks are very interested in taking their lives back and providing for their own basic needs. The superficiality of the Western lifestyle and modern convenience have left them dissatisfied, and they want more," she says.

Bad Seed opened its doors in 2009, the result of a productive 2-acre garden Salvaggio started in 2007. But the idea really had its seed in her quest for a life with meaning beyond a job and a house in the suburbs.

"I grew up in soulless suburbia with fertilized lawns, plastic bags and micro-

waves. I was unhappy and disillusioned as a teenager. I thought surely there must be something else," she says.

After she turned 18, Salvaggio traveled through the Mediterranean, Southeast Asia and the South Pacific, paying her way by working on organic farms for room and board. "That is how I discovered the undeniable connection one has with the land. It became obvious to me that growing food and providing for myself was the only way to feel satisfied and grounded in an otherwise consumer- obsessed, techno-industrial world," she says.

She and her husband, Daniel Heryer, grow a vast assortment of heirloom vegetables and herbs on their 2-acre plot at 95th Street and State Line Road. They feed themselves and sell the rest at Bad Seed, which is open 4:30 to 9 p.m. Fridays May 1 through Nov. 20.

Salvaggio is committed to urban agriculture for a variety of reasons, not the least of which is the smaller amount of energy it takes to get food from ground to table. Gardens also improve community interaction, nutrition, environmental awareness, food awareness, self-awareness and exercise, she says. And the food tastes better.

"We are concerned with the whole picture. One cannot be disconnected from the other," she says. "Self-reliance promotes a healthy environment and ultimately happiness: peace of mind, body and spirit."

What would an ideal world look like to Salvaggio? For one thing, the farmers market would die "because all my customers will be enjoying the bounty of their own organic garden — listening to the birds and staying the hell away from the supermarket!"

LEW EDMISTER RECLAIMS BLIGHTED SITE

About 2001, Lew Edmister looked at a debris-strewn vacant lot across from his apartment on Kansas City's West Side and had an idea. He contacted the property owners, got their backing and went to work.

The result: Fresh food for Edmister and his vegetable-buying customers and the removal of a local eyesore.

"It's a nontraditional garden," he says. "I grow art as well as food."

Edmister is on the board of the Kansas City Center for Urban Agriculture, which promotes gardening in vacant lots as a way to beautify the city, help the environment

and get healthy fresh foods into urban areas. He sells produce from the courtyard of his apartment and at a Friday evening farmers market near downtown Kansas City.

Building the garden has taken an enormous amount of work. The site was filled with broken bricks and cinder blocks, mortar chips, pipes and concrete. Some was

A wall in Edmister's garden is made of recycled radiators. Opposite: Lew Edmister.

hauled off, but Edmister salvaged quite a bit for use in the garden. He built retaining walls from concrete and masonry pieces to help level the sloped lot. (The landlord donated two or three truckloads of topsoil, he says.)

Debris also gives the garden an artistic touch. Pieces of iron radiator make up parts of the outside wall, and Edmister scavenged broken concrete from a Country Club Plaza fountain for visual interest. Against one side is a metal sculpture that was once a temporary installation at Powell Gardens. The north wall was a class project of decorative bricks made by students from the Kansas City Art Institute.

All that took time. The first year, Edmister says, he didn't grow much more than tomatoes, peppers and okra to feed himself or give away. Now he grows enough vegetables on his plot to provide for himself and sell some to people in the neighborhood.

Chapter 17:
Our favorite resources

After 25 years, we know a lot about gardening, but not everything. Here's where we turn when we want to learn more:

ONLINE

Johnson County Extension Master Gardeners
Hotline: (913) 715-7050
Home page: www.johnson.ksu.edu/DesktopDefault.aspx?tabid=106
E-mail: garden.help@jocogov.org

University of Missouri Extension Master Gardeners
Hotline: 816-833-8733
Home page: extension.missouri.edu/gkcmg
E-mail: kumarl@missouri.edu

National Gardening Association
www.garden.org/home

Sustainable Gardening with Susan Harris
www.sustainable-gardening.com

USDA COMPLETE GUIDE TO HOME CANNING

www.uga.edu/nchfp/publications/usda/2_USDAcanningGuide1_06.pdf

BOOKS

Organic gardening

Rodale's Ultimate Encyclopedia of Organic Gardening: The Indispensable Green Resource for Every Gardener by Fern Marshall Bradley (Rodale Books, revised 2009)

Rodale's Illustrated Encyclopedia of Organic Gardening by Maria Rodale (DK Publishing, 2005)

The New Victory Garden by Bob Thomson (Little, Brown & Co., 1987)

Seed saving

Seed to Seed: Seed Saving and Growing Techniques for Vegetable Gardeners by Suzanne Ashworth (Seed Savers Exchange, 2002)

Saving Seeds: The Gardener's Guide to Growing and Storing Vegetable and Flower Seeds by Marc Rogers (Storey Publishing, revised 1991)

Canning and food processing

Complete Guide to Home Canning, by the U.S. Department of Agriculture

Ball Blue Book of Preserving (Ball Corp. 100th anniversary edition)

Root Cellaring: Natural Cold Storage of Fruits and Vegetables by Mike Bubel and Nancy Bubel (Storey Publishing, 1991)

GARDENING COMMUNITY, BLOGS AND CLASSES

Garden Rant: www.gardenrant.com

Kansas City Center for Urban Agriculture: www.kccua.org

Kansas City Community Gardens: www.kccg.org

kcgardens.kansascity.com

Powell Gardens: www.powellgardens.blogspot.com

UMKC Communiversity: www.umkc.edu/commu

The Bad Seed: www.badseedfarm.com

The Savvy Gardener: www.savvygardener.com

And please come visit us at our blog, Mike & Roxie's Vegetable Paradise: **roxiemike.wordpress.com**

PHOTO CREDITS

Here are the sources for the photographs and illustrations in *Mike & Roxie's Vegetable Paradise*:

Aaron Leimkuehler, *The Kansas City Star:* Pages 7, 8, 9, 10, 16, 22, 25, 30, 32, 35, 52, 56, 59, 64, 68, 73, 82, 85, 87, 89, 90, 93, 100, 102, 103, 112, 116, 119, 120, 123, 131, 132.

Mike Hendricks & Roxie Hammill: Pages 12, 14, 15, 18, 21, 48, 50, 61, 63, 106, 114, 126, 127.

Lon Eric Craven: Pages 44, 47, 51, 67, 80.

Kansas City Star archives: Pages 5, 33, 43, 71, 96, 125.

photos.com: Pages 19, 26, 27, 28, 31, 34, 36, 37, 39, 54, 72, 74, 76, 78, 95, 98, 99, 104, 109, 111, 115.

istockphoto.com: Pages 40, 96.

Front cover: Aaron Leimkuehler, istockphoto.com, photos.com
Back cover: Aaron Leimkuehler, photos.com